ALL THE WORDS

A YEAR OF READING ABOUT WRITING

KRISTEN TATE

Copyright © 2020 by Kristen Tate

All rights reserved.

No part of this book may be reproduced in any form or by any electronic or mechanical means, including information storage and retrieval systems, without written permission from the author, except for the use of brief quotations in a book review.

ISBN: 978-1-7345742-0-3 (Ebook)
ISBN: 978-1-7345742-1-0 (Paperback)
ISBN: 978-1-7345742-2-7 (Hardback)

Published by The Blue Garret
www.thebluegarret.com

Cover design by Rachel Metzger
Proofreading by Kelly Cozy, Bookside Manner

To Ryan, who invited me into the Blue Garret

CONTENTS

Author's Note	ix
Week 1 *Have a Plan—Hold It Lightly*	1
Week 2 *Anne Lamott, Bird by Bird*	3
Week 3 *Stephen King, On Writing*	7
Week 4 *Lisa Cron, Wired for Story*	11
Week 5 *E. M. Forster, Aspects of the Novel*	14
Week 6 *Elizabeth Gilbert, Big Magic*	18
Week 7 *Shawn Coyne, The Story Grid, Part I*	21
Week 8 *Shawn Coyne, The Story Grid, Part 2*	24
Week 9 *Fill the Well*	27
Week 10 *Natalie Goldberg, Writing Down the Bones*	31
Week 11 *Benjamin Dreyer, Dreyer's English*	34
Week 12 *Susan Bell, The Artful Edit*	37
Week 13 *Among the Word Nerds*	41
Week 14 *Jessica Brody, Save the Cat! Writes a Novel*	44
Week 15 *Renni Browne and Dave King, Self-Editing for Fiction Writers*	47
Week 16 *Chuck Wendig, Damn Fine Story*	51
Week 17 *Constance Hale, Sin and Syntax*	55
Week 18 *Jane Smiley, 13 Ways of Looking at the Novel*	58

Week 19 *Twyla Tharp, The Creative Habit*	64
Week 20 *Janet Burroway, Writing Fiction*	68
Week 21 *James Frey, How to Write a Damn Good Mystery*	74
Week 22 *Janice Hardy, Revising Your Novel*	80
Week 23 *A Pause*	83
Week 24 *Brian Shawver, The Language of Fiction*	84
Week 25 *Ursula K. Le Guin, Steering the Craft*	88
Week 26 *Craft Book Taxonomy*	92
Week 27 *How to Read a Book*	95
Week 28 *K. M. Weiland, Outlining Your Novel*	99
Week 29 *James Scott Bell, Write Your Novel from the Middle*	102
Week 30 *Jane Alison, Meander, Spiral, Explode*	105
Week 31 *Dean Wesley Smith, Writing into the Dark*	108
Week 32 *June Casagrande, It Was the Best of Sentences, It Was the Worst of Sentences*	111
Week 33 *Francine Prose, Reading Like a Writer*	114
Week 34 *Christopher Castellani, The Art of Perspective*	117
Week 35 *David Lynch, Catching the Big Fish*	121
Week 36 *Jack Bickham, Elements of Fiction Writing*	125
Week 37 *Elizabeth George, Write Away*	128
Week 38 *Walter Mosley, Elements of Fiction*	133
Week 39 *Steven Pinker, The Sense of Style*	136

Week 40 — 141
John Gardner, The Art of Fiction

Week 41 — 147
Meredith Maran, Why We Write

Week 42 — 150
Jessica Morrell, Thanks, but This Isn't for Us

Week 43 — 154
Charles Johnson, The Way of the Writer

Week 44 — 159
Donald Maas, Writing the Breakout Novel

Week 45 — 163
John Truby, The Anatomy of Story

Week 46 — 166
Virginia Tufte, Artful Sentences

Week 47 — 171
Sandra Scofield, The Last Draft

Week 48 — 175
Helen Corner-Bryant and Kathryn Price, On Editing

Week 49 — 178
Brooks Landon, Building Great Sentences

Book Recommendations — 183
Books Reviewed — 188

Also by Kristen Tate — 193
Acknowledgments — 195
About the Author — 197
Notes — 199

AUTHOR'S NOTE

This little book originated in a series of weekly email newsletters I wrote and sent over the course of 2019. I've retained the week-by-week format of the original because writing itself happens across weeks and seasons. There will be ups and downs, starts and stops, stalls and bursts in any creative life—certainly there were in mine as I was writing these essays. The book is about reading, but it's also about writing, about what it feels like to sustain a creative project over the course of a year.

You could start reading at week one and go straight through to week forty-nine over the course of a year, or you could browse around, looking for what you need right now. There is an alphabetized list of all of the books reviewed at the end of this volume, along with a list of book recommendations tailored to specific writing problems or situations. When you find something that resonates with you, I encourage you to read more of the books I've referenced; I've only scratched the surface of what these writers have to offer.

Wherever you are on your journey, I hope this book will

AUTHOR'S NOTE

be a companion and an inspiration when you need it. Every week is week one—a new chance to start, to learn something new, to experience the world, to write.

Kristen Tate
January 5, 2020

WEEK 1
HAVE A PLAN—HOLD IT LIGHTLY

It's week one of a new year. I usually work in my home office, but I'm writing this at my kitchen table. It's a windy, wintry day in San Francisco. Out the kitchen window, I can see that the seagulls have come inland from the ocean to wheel around the nearby park, which means we're in for a gorgeous gusty rainstorm. I'm not quite ready to get back to work after my holiday break, and I'm not quite ready to categorize this writing as work. Perhaps it will become a weekly task to be crossed off a list, but right now it feels fresh—more like play than work.

I love the start of a new year and the excitement of new plans and projects. The project of this book is to embark on a year-long tour of writing craft books. Many of them are old favorites I will be rereading, and others are either new or new to me. In previous years, I've fit writing into little gaps in my schedule, which has resulted in sporadic bursts of blog posts but not much else. This year, I've scheduled big chunks of writing time into my week, and I'm excited to see what might emerge. By scheduling the time but not prescribing the outcome, I'm following the wise advice of Frank Ostaseski, the cofounder of the Zen Hospice Project:

Have a plan. Hold it lightly.[1]

I recently came across a passage from Thoreau's journal that also speaks to the power of making a start—any start:

> Each thought that is welcomed and recorded is a nest egg, by the side of which more will be laid. Thoughts accidentally thrown together become a frame in which more may be developed and exhibited . . . . Having by chance recorded a few disconnected thoughts and brought them into juxtaposition, they suggest a whole new field in which it was possible to labor and to think. Thought begat thought.[2]

As the writer and artist Austin Kleon points out in his riff on this passage, "a literal 'nest egg' is a real or fake egg that you put in a nest to encourage a bird or a hen to lay more eggs."[3] The nest egg doesn't need to be a fancy one; it can be a weeks-old supermarket egg from a huge industrial farm. *It doesn't even need to be a real egg.* You can go rummage around in your kid's junk drawer and find a tawdry plastic Easter egg to throw into that writing coop. The only important thing is that you do it.

Back to Kleon: "What Thoreau is saying is that by simply writing down a thought, you encourage more thoughts to come. When you have enough thoughts pushed together in the same space—a collage of thoughts, juxtaposed—they often lead to something totally new. This is the magic of writing."

This is the magic of writing. Simply make a start—any start—and see what happens. It's week one. What do you want to start?

WEEK 2
ANNE LAMOTT, BIRD BY BIRD

It's week two of the new year. Have you settled back into work, creative and otherwise, after those long, drifty days at the end of December?

If you are feeling stuck, empty, or maybe even dismayed at your stupid shiny resolutions for the new year, then Anne Lamott's *Bird by Bird: Some Instructions on Writing and Life* may be just the tonic you need. (Possibly you also need some cranberry shrub, in which case throw a few handfuls of fresh cranberries into a glass jar along with a cup of apple cider vinegar and a half-cup each of sugar and water. Maybe toss in a few cloves or a cinnamon stick or even a spoonful of peppercorns. Stick it in the back of the fridge and rediscover it in a few days.)

Lamott does not pretend that writing is easy or fun. "Writing can be a pretty desperate endeavor, because it is about some of our deepest needs: our need to be visible, to be heard, our need to make sense of our lives, to wake up and grow and belong," she tells us. Think about how hard it is to do any one of those things: to have a clear-eyed view of your place in the world, to continue to develop and change, to be part of a community you have found and nourished.

But wait, it gets worse. To do this work, writers often need to confront the extremes of human emotion:

> We write to expose the unexposed. If there is one door in the castle you have been told not to go through, you must. Otherwise, you'll just be rearranging furniture in rooms you've already been in. Most human beings are dedicated to keeping that one door shut. But the writer's job is to see what's behind it, to see the bleak unspeakable stuff, and to turn the unspeakable into words—not just into any words but if we can, into rhythm and blues.

If this door-opening business sounds grim, Lamott has much to say about the rewards. Writing, she says, is "spiritually invigorating" and "intellectually quickening"—"a perfect focus for life." Writing is also an act of generosity. Giving your book to readers is like throwing a party, being the person who orchestrates a night of cranberry shrub cocktails (throw some bourbon and ice into that concoction waiting in the back of the fridge!) and Bananagrams on a dark winter night for no reason at all. As Lamott says, "It is one of the greatest feelings known to humans, the feeling of being the host. Of hosting people, of being the person to whom they come for food and drink and company. This is what the writer has to offer."

Bird by Bird can remind you why you wanted to start writing in the first place, and it can also help you make forward progress when you are stalled. One of my favorite insights in the book is about writer's block: "The word block suggests that you are constipated or stuck, when the truth is that you're empty." Instead of staring at a blank page or screen, try filling yourself back up—go out into the world and see a movie or visit a museum or just sit on a park bench and watch what all of the humans around you are up to and then come back to the page with new sensory experiences and insights in your writing well.

Lamott's best lesson, though, is that writers need to lower their standards for themselves at the beginning of a project. This can be hard—you are a writer, after all, because you love words, and you particularly love the way that words, lined up just so, can produce surprise, suspense, insight, and joy. You need to forget about all of that when you are starting a project. Lamott admits, "The only way I can get anything written at all is to write really, really shitty first drafts." To achieve that shitty first draft, writers must slay the dragon of perfectionism: "Go ahead and make big scrawls and mistakes. Use up lots of paper.... We need to make messes in order to find out who we are and why we are here—and, by extension, what we're supposed to be writing." They are called *rough* drafts for a reason, y'all.

Bird by Bird is a fundamentally positive book, and Lamott is honest and very, very funny. (My favorite one-liner: "Having a baby is like suddenly getting the world's worst roommate, like having Janis Joplin with a bad hangover and PMS come to stay with you." Truth.) Lamott writes traditionally published literary fiction and memoirs, and her perspective is very much shaped by those parameters, but I think it's a book that all writers can benefit from.

I'll leave you with one more gem you can revisit when the page is blank and the well is dry and those doors seem impossible to open: "Writing has so much to give, so much to teach, so many surprises. That thing you had to force yourself to do—the actual act of writing—turns out to be the best part. It's like discovering that while you thought you needed the tea ceremony for the caffeine, what you really needed was the tea ceremony. The act of writing turns out to be its own reward." Show up for the ceremony of writing this week and try to make a mess.

WEEK 3
STEPHEN KING, ON WRITING

It is week three. Have you returned to a comfortable writing routine? Or are you still on pause, waiting for a reason to begin? Perhaps your story just hasn't found you yet. As Stephen King points out in *On Writing*, you can't just go out and dig one up:

> There is no Idea Dump, no Story Central, no Island of the Buried Bestsellers; good story ideas seem to come quite literally from nowhere, sailing at you right out of the empty sky: two previously unrelated ideas come together and make something new under the sun. Your job isn't to find these ideas but to recognize them when they show up.

His advice for what to do while you are waiting for that story to come sailing up to you? Read. Read and read and read, especially in the genre in which you want to write: "The real importance of reading is that it creates an ease and intimacy with the process of writing; one comes to the country of the writer with one's papers and identification pretty much in order."

This is sound advice, as is King's advice for what to do when that idea does arrive: write with the door closed, he says, and then revise with the door open. This is another version of Anne Lamott's wisdom about really shitty first drafts. Keep the door closed, keep the writing private, and find out what is going to happen to your characters before you start showing your work to others.

And how does King start the writing itself? "The situation comes first. The characters—always flat and unfeatured, to begin with—come next. Once these things are fixed in my mind, I begin to narrate." It's the characters who tell him where the plot of the piece will go, not the other way around. The situation may come sailing up to you, fully formed, but what comes next, during the narration, is slow and painstaking: "Stories are relics, part of an undiscovered pre-existing world. The writer's job is to use the tools in his or her toolbox to get as much of each one out of the ground intact as possible."

After that excavation is complete, King puts the draft aside, still without showing it to anyone. ("Give yourself a chance to think," he says, "while the story is still like a field of freshly fallen snow, absent of any tracks save your own.") King advises letting it rest for at least six weeks, so that when you come back to the draft, it will be "like reading the work of someone else, a soul-twin, perhaps." This gap will allow you to see holes in the plot or in the character development, and it will make it easier to kill off characters or plot points or excessive description. (The famous advice to "murder your darlings" is often attributed to King, but King adapted it, as he notes, from the British writer Arthur Quiller-Couch, whose 1916 book *On the Art of Writing* was one of the first modern writing craft books.)

Only after King has uncovered the story does he begin looking for "underlying patterns"—the symbolism, the theme, the meaning he wants to make of the story—and bring them out in subsequent drafts. At this point, King advises, you can open the door and start showing the manuscript to people you trust, who can tell you when something has missed the mark.

Let's go back to that toolbox King mentioned—the one writers have with them when they are excavating their story. King has an actual toolbox in mind to anchor this metaphor, a huge, heavy, custom-built toolbox that belonged to his grandfather, Fazza: "It had three levels, the top two removable, all three containing little drawers as cunning as Chinese boxes." Your common tools should go on top, King tells us, and these include vocabulary and grammar. He gives us a few tips about how to use these tools: use active rather than passive verbs; allow yourself an occasional sentence fragment; restrict yourself to simple forms of dialogue attribution (like *he said*); and avoid adverbs, for they are "not your friends." (King is, I imagine, responsible for the slaughter of untold manuscript adverbs.)

King then allows the metaphor to dwindle away before we get to see past that first level of the toolbox. We never get to peek inside the cunning drawers where King keeps his more specialized tools. I was disappointed at first when I realized this, and I attributed it to what King tells us in the last part of the book—that this section was written while he was, with great difficulty and pain, finding his way back to writing after being struck by a van and almost losing his life.

But when I thought about it further, I realized that it wouldn't help you or me for King to show us his tools in any greater detail. The ones that work best for him are those he has made his own—the ones that fit just right in the customized compartments hidden away in his toolbox. This is something I want you to remember throughout this year as

I lay out a veritable hardware store of shiny new tools in front of you: the tool is not your own until you use it.

I'll leave you this week with one more bit of wisdom from *On Writing*. King wrote his early books in tiny nooks, cramming a desk in wherever it would fit, while dreaming of having a big desk in a dedicated writing room. "In 1981 I got the one I wanted and placed it in the middle of a spacious, skylighted study . . . . For six years I sat behind that desk either drunk or wrecked out of my mind, like a ship's captain in charge of a voyage to nowhere." After getting sober, King got rid of the "T. rex desk" and put a couch in its place, so his kids could come up and watch a movie or ballgame. He got a smaller desk and put it in the corner. "I'm sitting under it now, a fifty-three-year-old man with bad eyes, a gimp leg, and no hangover. I'm doing what I know how to do, and as well as I know how to do it. . . . It starts with this: put your desk in the corner, and every time you sit down there to write, remind yourself why it isn't in the middle of the room. Life isn't a support-system for art. It's the other way around."

I think we all have our fantasy versions of that enormous desk in the giant skylit space—that place where the words will flow onto the page like magic. It's a place that is just for us, our room of one's own, and it has a door that's shut. But closing the metaphorical door to your first draft shouldn't extend to locking yourself away from the world. When you close yourself off from the life and world around you and seal yourself inside your own brain—which is one way to think about addiction—you also seal yourself off from seeing the human beings around you, and they are the ones who will show you what your characters will do and what your book is about and why you are writing it in the first place.

WEEK 4
LISA CRON, WIRED FOR STORY

It is week four. I've settled into the pleasant routine of writing these reviews each week, and I'm beginning to contemplate what's next. I think I'm almost ready to open up the drafts of my two barely begun novels and see what's what.

This week's craft book, Lisa Cron's *Wired for Story: The Writer's Guide to Using Brain Science to Hook Readers from the Very First Sentence*, made that moment feel a little bit more daunting because Cron is a firm believer in advance plotting and, y'all, I'm a pantser. I generally show up to the page with a direction and a few ideas about stops along the way and then feel my way forward bit by bit.

Cron points out that this approach often leads to stories that meander around rather than build: "Without a premeditated destination based on the battle between the protagonist's inner issue and his longstanding desire, they wander, taking the scenic route to who-knows-where." I think this is an accurate assessment, and certainly I agree with her that if you can figure out that destination before you begin writing, then you are likely to arrive at a solid draft much faster than if you just pants along.

However, I disagree with Cron's assertion that the route cannot be straightened out during the revision process. "New material," she says, "is crafted first and foremost with an eye toward how it will fit into what's already there, because our unconscious allegiance is to what we've already written, rather than to the story itself. Ironically, the 'new' draft is often a big step backward—what was flat in the prior version remains flat, now it just makes less sense." Sure, that can happen, but it means the revision hasn't been thorough enough, not that effective revision is impossible. I've worked with many authors who have had to unstitch large sections of their narrative and then weave new material into the resulting holes, with magical results. Just this week, I talked to an author who needed to create a believable character motivation for a crucial plot point. Her solution took my breath away: it not only explained the actions of the character, it also injected suspense in another area of the plot. I don't think the author could have come to this brilliant, layered solution in an earlier draft because she couldn't yet see how all of the pieces of her complex narrative fit together.

So, in summary, if you can see your story and your characters clearly enough to outline, then by all means follow Cron's suggestions. When you are sketching out your character bios, Cron advises you to look for "the event in his past that knocked his worldview out of alignment, triggering the internal issue that keeps him from achieving his goal; and the inception of his desire for the goal itself." This is exactly right, and you'll be ahead of the game if you identify these elements before you've written a word. But if you have to write a meandering first draft in order to figure them out, don't despair.

Cron's stance on outlining and revision aside, I think *Wired for Story* is an invaluable resource for novelists. Cron draws on neuroscience to support her advice, and while that's a nice extra, it's largely irrelevant in my opinion. Neuroscience might provide the *why*, but readers are really going to be looking for the *what* and the *how*, and Cron provides these in spades. She covers the most important aspects of storytelling: how to make your characters' goals drive the plot; how to harness the power of conflict and cause and effect; how to use setting details effectively; how and when to use flashbacks and backstory.

Her advice is sound, supported by plentiful examples, and masterfully organized. Particularly useful are the checklists at the end of each chapter. Have you finished a first draft and want to figure out the strengths and weaknesses of your manuscript? Working through these checklists, on your own or with a critique partner, would be an excellent way to go.

I'll leave you with Cron's definition of story:

> A story is how what happens affects someone who is trying to achieve what turns out to be a difficult goal, and how he or she changes as a result. . . . As counterintuitive as it may sound, a story is not about the plot or even what happens in it. Stories are about how we, rather than the world around us, change. They grab us only when they allow us to experience how it would feel to navigate the plot. Thus story, as we'll see throughout, is an internal journey, not an external one.

Set off all of your beautiful plot meteors—your dead bodies, your dreamy romances, your family dramas, your epic battles—but don't forget that it is your protagonist who is the bright sun at the center of your story galaxy.

WEEK 5
E. M. FORSTER, ASPECTS OF THE NOVEL

It is week five. How is the writing going? I've just shelved a piece of business-related writing I had been trying to check off my to-do list because I could not find a voice for it that felt both professional and authentic. I'm going to let it sulk in its Google folder for a few days while I turn to this weekly essay, where I'm beginning to feel at home.

If you were an English major, you might have encountered E. M. Forster's *Aspects of the Novel* in college. Perhaps, like me, you read the "People (continued)" chapter, ruthlessly severed from the "People" chapter and bound into a photocopied course reader, and learned Forster's distinction between "flat" and "round" characters. (Refresher: if a character changes, or is capable of change, it is round. If not, it is flat.) You might have also encountered Forster's distinction between story and plot. Both are "a narrative of events," he tells us, but a story focuses on sequence (the *what next*), while a plot focuses on causality (the *why*). "'The king died and then the queen died' is a story. 'The king died, and then the queen died of grief' is a plot. The time-sequence is preserved, but the sense of causality overshadows it."

Through most of this slim volume, Forster sticks to definitions. He wants to tell us what a novel is rather than how to write one—a choice that makes sense when we consider his original audience. *Aspects of the Novel* originated in a series of lectures Forster gave at Trinity College, Cambridge, in 1927. To us, English literature seems like one of the pillars of academia, but to Forster and his audience, it was a newcomer to the university—Cambridge did not establish an English department until 1919. Forster was speaking, first and foremost, to academics, not practitioners. So if you want to know more about how to create round characters or transform a story into a plot, I'd direct you back to Lisa Cron's *Wired for Story*, which I discussed last week, because you are not going to find instruction in *Aspects of the Novel*.

Forster himself would have, I think, agreed with Cron's advice about how to create living, breathing, rounded characters. And this, to Forster, is the real value of the novel as a form: "We cannot understand each other, except in a rough and ready way; we cannot reveal ourselves even when we want to; what we call intimacy is only a makeshift; perfect knowledge is an illusion. But in the novel we can know people perfectly, and, apart from the general pleasure of reading, we can find here a compensation for their dimness in life." If you want to take a pleasant detour at this point, by all means procure and read Forster's novels *A Room with a View* and *Howards End*. A further instructive detour would be to watch the Merchant Ivory films of the novels and identify the storytelling tools particular to fiction and to film. (Hint: look for interiority and narrative summary in the novels, and think about whether, and how, the filmmakers transmit these moments.)

Forster may know his characters perfectly, but as a writer, he still finds it difficult to control them:

The characters arrive when evoked, but full of the spirit of mutiny. For they have these numerous parallels with people like ourselves, they try to live their own lives and are consequently often engaged in treason against the main scheme of the book. They "run away," they "get out of hand" they are creations inside a creation, and often inharmonious towards it; if they are given complete freedom they kick the book to pieces, and if they are kept too sternly in check, they revenge themselves by dying, and destroy it by intestinal decay.

Forster, I'm guessing, was also a pantser.

If he is pessimistic on the subject of character, Forster approaches existential despair on the subject of plot: "After all, why has a novel to be planned? Cannot it grow? Why need it close, as a play closes? Cannot it open out? Instead of standing above his work and controlling it, cannot the novelist throw himself into it and be carried along to some goal that he does not foresee? The plot is exciting and may be beautiful, yet is it not a fetish, borrowed from the drama, from the spatial limitations of the stage? Cannot fiction devise a framework that is not so logical yet more suitable to its genius?" Hoping to find that alternative framework, Forster examines André Gide's *Les Faux-monnayeurs* but finds it to be only "various bundles of words." Later in this book, in week thirty, we'll see that Jane Alison brings a similar question to the novel but with more promising results.

By 1927, when he gave these lectures, Forster had published five novels, including *A Room with a View* (1908), *Howards End* (1910), and *A Passage to India* (1924). He died in 1970 without ever having completed another. Did he sense in 1927 that this would be the case? I think he might have. I can almost picture him, surveying the collection of perfectly round characters he had created, unable to let them run loose but unwilling to draw the noose of plot around their necks.

Depressing to contemplate? Yes, if, like me, you wish Forster had managed to write his way out of that conundrum. But for yourself as a writer, I don't think it needs to be. Here's Forster himself, near the end of *Aspects of the Novel*, to tell you why:

> Perhaps our subject, namely the books we have read, has stolen away from us while we theorize, like a shadow from an ascending bird. The bird is all right—it climbs, it is consistent and eminent. The shadow is all right—it has flickered across roads and gardens. But the two things resemble one another less and less, they do not touch as they did when the bird rested its toes on the ground. Criticism, especially a critical course, is so misleading. However lofty its intentions and sound its method, its subject slides away from beneath it, imperceptibly away, and lecturer and audience may awake with a start to find that they are carrying on in a distinguished and intelligent manner, but in regions which have nothing to do with anything they have read.

Maybe read a novel, Forster is telling his audience, *instead of listening to me talk about them*. Remember this as we continue to examine theories about what, how, and why to write a novel. These theories and practices may help you—I hope that they will. But if you get overwhelmed or stuck, pick up a favorite novel and see what it has to teach you.

WEEK 6
ELIZABETH GILBERT, BIG MAGIC

It is week six. I managed to write myself out of that tangle I was in last week. It was just a simple little job description, and I had expected it to take maybe an hour. But an evil little demon called imposter syndrome snuck in and started whispering, *Who do you think you are, acting like a boss?* And that's all it took to stop the words—or to stop them from sounding like mine.

Reading Elizabeth Gilbert's *Big Magic: Creative Living beyond Fear* this week helped me shake off that demon by reminding me that I can and do give myself permission to be a business owner—and a boss. Sure, I've got an official-looking business registration certificate from the city of San Francisco and an editing certification in a file folder in my office and even a fancy, framed PhD diploma sitting somewhere in the garage. I've got a website and a logo and some cool business cards. But none of these things gave me permission to start—and now to expand—an editing business. That was something I had to give myself.

And that's Gilbert's key message for creators of all kinds: "You do not need anybody's permission to live a creative life."

You also, she tells us, don't need to have a degree. You don't need to be independently wealthy, and you don't need a studio "wife" to keep all of life's mundanities away. You don't need to be in thrall to the dark demons of addiction. You don't need to suffer to be creative.

What do you need? According to Gilbert, "The essential ingredients for creativity remain exactly the same for everybody: courage, enchantment, permission, persistence, trust—and those elements are universally accessible. Which does not mean that creative living is always easy; it merely means that creative living is always *possible*."

The book is organized around these five ingredients, making it easy to absorb a dose of whatever it is you happen to need at the time. And I think that's what *Big Magic* is: a creative medicine cabinet that you can use to diagnose and treat any number of ills. If the words are stuck or you are paralyzed by doubt or you feel dull and uninspired, spend some time with this book. (The audiobook version, narrated by Gilbert herself, is particularly good company.)

I didn't put *Big Magic* on the schedule for this week because I was stuck—in fact, I hadn't recognized my stuckness as a problem Gilbert could help me with—but because I wanted to imagine Gilbert in conversation with the other writers I've looked at so far. Anne Lamott, Stephen King, and E. M. Forster all treat inspiration as a black hole that is impossible to even see clearly, much less explore. You must dive in anyway, they seem to tell us, and if you are lucky, you will be magically transported to another galaxy and bring your readers with you. If you aren't lucky—well, you might find yourself drifting aimlessly in that empty space of existential despair where we left Forster last week.

Part of the magic of *Big Magic* is that Gilbert acknowledges the mystery of the creative process but refuses to be frightened by it. She has even learned to enjoy the trickster side of creativity. One of her most memorable stories is about deciding to abandon an idea for a novel only to see a very similar idea turned into a successful novel by another writer. Gilbert could have responded with paranoia and envy. Instead, she finds the coincidence delightful—proof of her belief that creativity is mystical, transcendent, divine, "a force of enchantment not entirely human in its origins."

This belief guides the way Gilbert approaches her work. She cultivates curiosity, staying open to the ideas flitting around her, and she sits down and does the writing. Inspiration, Gilbert says, "will come and go, and you must let it come and go." You must "let go of the addiction to creative suffering" and approach the work with "stubborn gladness" and "a fierce sense of personal entitlement."

Cultivating that sense of personal entitlement will allow you to insist on the time and space you need to do the work. Remind yourself, every day, that *you have permission to be a writer*. I am not giving you permission because you already have it—it is your birthright. But I am reminding you.

WEEK 7
SHAWN COYNE, THE STORY GRID, PART I

It is week seven. How are the words treating you this week? Tenderly, I hope, in honor of Valentine's Day. If not, kick 'em to the curb and throw their cheap, stale drugstore chocolates after them. Maybe learn some new words? In a different language even? Here are a few Italian words I prize: *eccoci qua* (here we are), *allora* (well, then), and *piano, piano* (slowly, slowly). As Italians know, they fit nicely into conversational gaps, especially when accompanied by an insouciant shrug.

Now, let's get down to the Serious Business of Story. One glance at *The Story Grid: What Good Editors Know* will show you that Shawn Coyne takes Story very seriously indeed, or at least that's the implication of his capitalization style. But you'll have to get over the capitalization because I think this book is worth your attention if you are a novelist.

Coyne treats a novel the way an arachnologist might treat an unfamiliar spider: he pins it to a board to be anatomized and taxonomized. Is this process pretty or inspirational? Not particularly. But it's very useful. Even when you disagree with some of his classifications and conclusions, you will find yourself exploring aspects of the novel you hadn't given much thought to before.

There is a lot to learn from this book, but here are a few of the insights I have found most helpful as an editor:

- Most novels have both an "external content genre" and an "internal content genre." The external genre is often defined by a convention: to find a satisfying relationship in romance, to solve the murder in a mystery. The internal genre often explores the protagonist's subconscious needs and desires. Setting up a cause-and-effect relationship between the two genres provides a powerful engine for your plot. (This is the territory Lisa Cron takes us through in *Wired for Story*, which I reviewed in week four.)
- Look for a turning point in your scene—either an action or a revelation that creates change. If you can't find one, you likely don't need the scene. If you've got too many of one kind (all action or all revelation), you should introduce more variety.
- A novel can be broken down into three phases: "the beginning is all about hooking your reader . . . getting them so deeply curious and involved in the Story that there is no way they'll abandon it until they know how it turns out. The middle is about building progressive complications that bring the stress and pressure down so hard on your lead character(s) that they are forced to take huge risks so that they can return to 'normal.' The ending is the big payoff, when the promises you've made from your hook get satisfied in completely unique and unexpected ways."

- There are five core elements to every story: an inciting incident, progressive complications, a crisis that requires a choice, a climax that results from the choice, and a resolution.
- There are three basic categories of conflict: inner conflict between the protagonist and their own brain (familiar, anyone?), interpersonal conflict between the protagonist and another character, and extrapersonal conflict between the protagonist and a natural force or society at large. Varying the kinds of conflict from scene to scene can help you build momentum and excitement.

If you do decide to venture into *The Story Grid*, I'd like to warn you against getting caught up in the labels (and there are a lot of them). Novels, after all, are not spiders, and they resist easy classification. And in certain moments, analysis can be harmful. When you are writing along on a magic carpet of inspiration and your story is just working (something I believe you can often know by instinct), you don't need classifications. You just need to keep writing. But when you have finished a draft or when you get stuck mid-draft, the taxonomies can become powerful tools that will show you where to go next.

WEEK 8
SHAWN COYNE, THE STORY GRID, PART 2

It is week eight. How was your week in writing? Were the words stubborn or shy, or did they come skipping right out of your brain and onto the page?

Writers have a lot of problems with words—coaxing them out, controlling their erratic behavior, choosing which ones to axe and which ones to spare. But for novelists, I think the biggest problem may be that there are so very many of them. Masses of words. Giant heaping piles of words.

This is one reason novelists often resist revision. It's impossible to see around to the other sides of these piles of words to get a full picture of the landscape, and it takes so much effort to move a pile from one place to another with your tiny little garden trowel.

I sympathize. And, if you are my client, I am going to tell you to polish up that little trowel and move the piles anyway because that's how you turn a mediocre novel into a good one or a good novel into a great one.

But before you start blindly flinging words around into different piles, I'm going to give you two more tools. Both of them are adapted from *The Story Grid* by Shawn Coyne, which we started discussing last week.

The first tool is a tall platform you can use to survey the entire domain of your novel. Once you see all of your piles from up above, you can start to evaluate what's working and what's not. Coyne calls this the "Foolscap Method," and his procedure involves identifying a series of key components that help define the boundaries of the book: the external and internal genre, the point of view, the key scenes. As an editor, I simplify this into something that looks like a summary or blurb of the book, and that might work better for you too. The key is to see the big picture of your book, however you get there.

Like Lisa Cron in *Wired for Story*, Coyne advises trying to fill in as much of this big picture as you can before you start writing. Unlike Cron, however, Coyne acknowledges that you will almost certainly have to revisit it after you finish your first draft. For example, did you break through the genre boundaries of the paranormal mystery plot you thought you were writing? If so, what do you want to do about it? If that romance path looks like a dead end from on top of your platform, then maybe you fill in the gap in your wall and let the forest grow back over the path. But if it takes just the right twist and leads straight back into your domain, maybe you want to redraw your borders to include it. These are the kind of big questions your platform will help you answer. (You might also be able to pick off an evil troll while you are up there.)

The second tool is a map with a gazetteer listing all of the places in your domain and the important things about them. This is the "Story Grid" of Coyne's title, and I think it's the most useful piece of the book. At its most basic, the Story Grid is simply a spreadsheet with a brief summary of each scene, along with a number of key facts about it. Coyne advises a method that I think is too exhaustive (and exhausting) for most books, so I advise you pick and choose which elements to include if you try this tool (and I think you should). I generally leave off the character columns in my spreadsheets, for example, but I often include a separate backstory column.

The value of this spreadsheet—your map and gazetteer—is that you can use it to evaluate the structural integrity of your various piles of words as well as see how these piles relate to one another and to the boundaries of your domain. Rather than painstakingly moving one of your giant piles from one place to another, only to find that it doesn't look great in the new spot either, you can make that assessment before the move and then execute it with confidence. You'll realize that the little hillock next to the new location needs to be shoveled in with your relocated pile and that the lopsided pile down the way needs to be carted off altogether. You can make a holistic, coherent revision plan for your whole book at one time, which will make the next draft dramatically better.

This is what the Story Grid can do for your own work, but I also think it makes an excellent learning tool. As Coyne puts it, "Just as to be a bodybuilder, you need to be a weightlifter first, to be a writer, you need to be a reader first." If you are just starting out as a novelist or if you are contemplating writing in a different genre, you can learn a tremendous amount by putting together a story spreadsheet for several novels to see how they work and what they have in common.

Coyne's tools can also be reassuring when you get buried in your piles of words and feel like you will never be able to shovel yourself out. "You as the writer are not the problem, the problem is the problem," Coyne reminds us. Use your brain and your tools and figure out how to solve it.

WEEK 9
FILL THE WELL

It is week nine. It's that tricky period when the shine of the new year has worn off and the calamitous Ides of March is looming. Whenever possible, I try to change my longitude or latitude at this time of year to shake up my routine and refill my creative well.

This year's trip—a meander through London and Edinburgh—was especially wonderful because inspiration for writers and readers is thick on the ground. Here are a few of my favorite discoveries.

At the Charles Dickens Museum in London, you can see the desk where Charles Dickens composed four million words, more or less. Nearby is a wall plaque with this quote: "Happiness is a gift and the trick is not to expect it but to delight in it when it comes."

When I sat down to check the accuracy and find the source of this quote (editing reflex!), I was surprised to learn, thanks to the work of "quotologist" Sue Brewton, that these words don't belong to Dickens at all but rather to Douglas McGrath, who wrote the screenplay for the 2002 film adaptation of Dickens's *Nicholas Nickleby*.[1] The museum doesn't explicitly attribute the quote to Dickens, but it is implied. Lesson: always check your quotes, y'all, or hire a copyeditor who will do it for you!

The Writer's Corner in Edinburgh's St. Giles' Cathedral includes a tribute to Margaret Oliphant, whose work was widely popular in the nineteenth century (she was reportedly Queen Victoria's favorite novelist) but little read today. Widowed early, she wrote a hundred books, mostly novels, and managed to support her three children with the income from her writing. She wrote in her memoir that her family "were quite pleased to magnify me, and proud of my work, but always with a hidden sense that it was an admirable joke, and no idea that any special facilities or retirement was necessary." I want to travel back in time and give her an office, with a door, and maybe give her children a stern lecture too.

Greyfriars Kirkyard, in Edinburgh's Old Town, was one place where I could feel and see all of the layers of the city's long literary history intersecting. Sir Walter Scott's characters regularly passed through this spot and, almost two hundred years later, J. K. Rowling found the names of two of her characters on the gravestones here.

The Writers' Museum in Edinburgh is full of delights (including a nineteenth-century printing press), but one of my favorite pieces was a sculpture that depicts a scene from Robert Louis Stevenson's novel *The Strange Case of Dr. Jekyll and Mr. Hyde*. It is one of a series that was left anonymously by the artist "in support of libraries, books, words and ideas." Even better, one of the materials used in the piece is a copy of Ian Rankin's second Rebus novel, *Hide and Seek*, which was inspired in part by Stevenson's novel.

The statue of Sir Walter Scott, topped by an elaborate Gothic tower, is one of the first sights you see when leaving Edinburgh's Waverley Station (itself named after one of his novels), but I preferred the bust of poet Hamish Henderson, made from the pages of his own books, which is tucked away in a corner of Sandy Bell's pub—a bottle of his favorite Lagavulin whisky beside him.

On my last night in London, I saw *The Curious Incident of the Dog in the Night-Time*, adapted from the novel by Mark Haddon. It's a remarkable adaptation, full of stage effects and movements that dramatize the inner experience of the protagonist, who has Asperger syndrome.

In a note in the program, Haddon comments that he now regrets that the phrase "Asperger syndrome" appeared on the cover of the novel when it was published. He prefers the protagonist's own description of himself as "someone who has Behavioural Problems." Haddon writes, "I like the way it gently mocks diagnostic medical language. I like the way it includes all of us (who doesn't have behavioural problems?). But I like it most of all because it is Christopher's own phrase. Labels tell us very little about the person who has been labelled and a lot about the people doing the labelling. If you want to find out who someone is, just ask them."

In a coincidence that I found thrilling, I discovered a very similar sentiment in the author interview at the end of Alex Reeve's *The House on Half Moon Street*, which I bought at Heathrow for the plane ride home with the last of my pounds. The novel is set in Victorian London, and the protagonist is a trans man. But, Reeve stresses in his interview, "this isn't a novel about being trans, this is a crime novel featuring a man who happens to be trans. Most characters in fiction seem to default to the so-called norm unless there's a plot-based reason for them not to. But the so-called norm isn't really normal at all. People come in lots of different flavours. Why should including a trans or gay or disabled or any other kind of character require the plot to centre around that attribute? I think we need to move beyond all that and include every kind of people in our stories as a matter of course." It takes bravery and sensitivity, but I wish more authors would follow the advice of Reeve and Haddon.

If the words are stuck or your mind is feeling dull, think about what you can do to shake things up and refill your well. You can keep it simple: a hike you've never done, a museum you haven't visited, a drive you've never taken, an afternoon at the library with a book you've never read. Almost anything works, as long as it involves novelty and motion. I think Elizabeth Gilbert is right here: "Any motion whatsoever beats inertia, because inspiration will always be drawn to motion." Get your blood stirring and your brain working, and creative magic will come flooding in.

WEEK 10
NATALIE GOLDBERG, WRITING DOWN THE BONES

It is week ten. Of all of the fifty-two weeks of the year, week ten might be my least favorite, followed closely by week nine and week eleven. My internal weather is always stormy in March. Here in San Francisco, it's been rainy and gray for weeks, and when the sun does make a brief appearance, it feels too sharp and bright.

Maybe it is the same for you? I hope not. I hope that you are sailing through calm seas under gentle blue skies and that the words are piling up in your document or notebook. But if not, I've got two tonics to offer you today, for this or whatever season you need them.

First, go out and get yourself a bag of lemons and a big knob of fresh ginger. Find a quiet hour, a vegetable peeler, a grater, and a sharp knife. Cut away the peel and pith of each lemon, then free each lemon segment from its membrane. Put the segments in a bowl or a food processor. Peel a big chunk of the ginger and grate it on top of the lemons. Whir the mixture in the food processor or crush and stir it together in the bowl, and then pour it into an ice cube tray and freeze. What you get are sunny yellow cubes so intense in flavor they will shock you right out of the dull gray fog blanketing your body and mind. Throw them in a cup of tea or a glass of seltzer or straight into your mouth.

Second, get yourself a copy of Natalie Goldberg's *Writing Down the Bones*, dip into it at random, and then do what she tells you: write for ten minutes without stopping or bring together a story circle or scramble the words of a few of your sentences and put them together again in an unexpected way. The book is full of suggestions—flip through it and you are sure to find one that speaks to you.

The central recommendation of the book is to commit to regular, timed writing practice that has no immediate goal or purpose. Set yourself an interval and then go: keep writing or typing, without stopping to reread or cross out or worry about grammar. "Lose control," Goldberg says. "Don't think. Don't get logical. Go for the jugular." Anne Lamott would add, "Make a mess."

The point is to write confidently, without fear, to show yourself you can do it. "Writing is the act of burning through the fog in your mind," Goldberg says. "Don't carry the fog out on paper. Even if you are not sure of something, express it as though you know yourself. With this practice you eventually will." I believe in the truth of Goldberg's words. Remember what Elizabeth Gilbert had to say about giving yourself permission to write? Goldberg takes it one step further and gives you permission to believe that you can create good work, even though "every time we begin, we wonder how we ever did it before. Each time is a new journey with no maps."

Goldberg is primarily a poet and memoirist, so she is able to mine this writing practice material directly when she turns to her more intentional creative work. If you are a novelist, you will uncover insights you can bring into your work, but you can also adapt her suggestions to explore your fictional world. Try doing some writing that won't end up in your novel but will help you know your characters and setting in a deeper way. Describe what March is like in the world of your novel. Tell a story from when your protagonist was eight years old or twelve or sixteen. Rewrite one of your scenes in second person ("you") or in first person plural ("we"). Imagine a day in the life of a minor character ten years after the events of your novel. The practice is the point. As Goldberg puts it, writing practice is "our wild forest where we gather energy before going to prune our garden, write our fine books and novels."

Writing Down the Bones is also a good companion whenever you are feeling March-ish because Goldberg believes down to her core that writing of any kind is healing work. Writing practice is, she says, "a way to help you penetrate your life and become sane." Writing is a way to confront our anxieties: "It's a measured way to dip yourself into that huge vast emptiness, that loss of control, and then pull yourself out so you can feel safe again." And writing is a way to celebrate the fact that "every minute we change": "At any point, we can step out of our frozen selves and our ideas and begin fresh. That is how writing is. Instead of freezing us, it frees us."

Goldberg tells the story of a group of students who had traveled a great distance to attend one of her courses for the fourth time, mostly to be reminded again that all they needed to do was "pick up a pen and write." So here is *your* reminder to do just that, in Goldberg's words: "In the middle of the world, make one positive step. In the center of chaos, make one definitive act. Just write. Say yes, stay alive, be awake. Just write. Just write. Just write."

WEEK 11
BENJAMIN DREYER, DREYER'S ENGLISH

It is week eleven. It has been a wrenching week in the world, and that can sometimes stop your words. Let yourself be silent or send your words elsewhere for a time, but then guide them gently back to your book. Books are solace, and we will need yours in the world someday, during other weeks that feel like this one.

Some of my happiest hours this week have been spent with the words of Benjamin Dreyer, the Random House copy chief, who has distilled his decades of experience in *Dreyer's English: An Utterly Correct Guide to Clarity and Style*. As you can sense from the title, Dreyer wears his wisdom lightly. He is quick to admit to his own crotchets and idiosyncrasies, and his advice is delivered with disarming humor. My favorite one-liner: "You are free to dislike such bureaucratese phrases as 'grow the economy' because they're, to use the technical term, icky." (Speaking of humor, the footnotes are not to be missed.)

Dreyer's English is not a grammar textbook (you will learn what a phrasal verb is, if you care to, but only by happenstance in the course of a discussion about title capitalization), nor is it an exhaustive reference book for writers or editors. Instead, it's a loosely organized tour through Dreyer's recommendations on common topics and his opinions about the "curiosities and arcana" that interest him. Wondering where Dreyer lands on the hot topics of editing? Here you go: first, "only godless savages eschew the series comma" (also known as the Oxford comma); second, "the singular 'they' is not the wave of the future; it's the wave of the present."

Writers of all stripes will benefit from his list of meaningless words and phrases to avoid (for example, *very, rather, really, quite, in fact*), as well as his chapter on "trimmables": phrases like *hollow tube* that are needlessly doubled. (My favorite of his examples in this chapter is *assless chaps*: "The garment, that is. Not fellows lacking in dorsal embonpoint. I'm not sure how often this will come up in your writing—or in your life—but chaps are, by definition, assless. Look at a cowboy. From behind.") His chapter on "confusables" is similarly valuable. I check *lead/led, desert/dessert, peak/peek/pique,* and *stationary/stationery* every time I see them pop up, and you should too. Even careful writers trip over these more often than you would think.

Seeing Dreyer demolish what he calls "the Great Nonrules of the English Language" is prime entertainment, and I look forward to citing his authority when there is an infinitive that needs to be split, a sentence that needs to be fragmented, or a list that needs to be introduced with "like."

Dreyer's chapter on fiction will be illuminating for novelists, and it's a must-read for fiction editors. You will search the *Chicago Manual of Style*, the style guide used by most book publishers, in vain for guidance on what to do "when characters self-interrupt and immediately resume speaking with a pronounced change in thought," but Dreyer has you covered: "I suggest the em dash–space–capital letter combo pack, thus: 'Our lesson for today is— No, we can't have class outside today, it's raining.'" His list of common consistency problems and his thoughts about dialogue are well worth a look, and his technique for seamlessly integrating flashbacks in past-tense narration is sheer brilliance: Cue the flashback by putting the first two or three verbs in the past perfect tense ("she had"), then shorten one or two more using the contracted form ("she'd"), and then "drop the past-perfecting altogether when no one's apt to be paying attention and slip into the simple past."

One of the lessons that I'd like writers to learn from *Dreyer's English* is that their editor is an ally, not an enemy. As Dreyer puts it, "The role of a copy editor is, above all else, to assist and enhance and advise rather than to correct—indeed, not to try to transform a book into the copy editor's notion of what a good book should be but, simply and with some measure of humility, to help fulfill an author's vision and make each book into the ideal version of itself." Hear, hear! (Not, as Dreyer reminds us, "here, here.")

I'll leave you this week with one final bit of wisdom from *Dreyer's English*: "Staring at words is always a bad idea. Stare at the word 'the' for more than ten seconds and reality begins to recede." If you experience this phenomenon, you know it's time to shut the tab or close the document or put down the pen and step away from the words for the day.

WEEK 12
SUSAN BELL, THE ARTFUL EDIT

It is week twelve. Spring has sprung, and the brain-wrecking jostle of the time jump in the US is behind us. This new season is a good time to evaluate your writing routine and make changes if you are stuck or the words feel stale. If you've been writing inside, get yourself outside. If you've been writing on a computer, grab a notebook and pen. If you've been writing in the mornings, try writing at night. Run an experiment for a week and see what happens.

This week's book, *The Artful Edit: On the Practice of Editing Yourself* by Susan Bell, is all about change—big change. If you've never substantially revised one of your drafts, or if you live in fear of being told (by an editor, a reader, or your own brain) that your manuscript needs major revision, this is the book to reach for.

The Artful Edit will not teach you the fundamentals of how to build a sound structure for your story (for that, turn back to Cron, week four, and Coyne, weeks seven and eight). What this book will do is show you how to enhance what you have—how to turn a crude shelter into a warm and inviting home.

Bell's most important point is that editing is a creative act, not a step in the publishing process that happens after a manuscript is mostly finished. If you approach your manuscript looking only for adverbs to slay, then that's all you will find. But if you step back and take a broader view, then you will be able to see incidents that can be foreshadowed or characters that can be further developed or images that can be turned into leitmotivs.

Editing provides the kind of psychological freedom that writing often cannot. In your first draft, you are still gathering your materials and creating your structure. When you are editing, you know what you are working with. As Bell puts it, "While we write into a void, we edit into a universe, however ravaged it may be. . . . So forget for a minute the intoxication of invention, and honor the cold splash relief of revision."

The most important step in the revision process is to learn how to approach your book as a reader and editor, rather than as a writer and creator. To do this, Bell explains, you must get some distance from your manuscript, and she provides a number of specific strategies for achieving this:

- Don't read and revise as you write your first draft so that you can come back to it with fresh eyes when you finish. Alternatively, put it in a drawer for some period of time after you finish and don't look at it.
- Read aloud. This is common advice, but Bell's wording of it will stick with you: "Intoned, your text becomes dynamic, whereas inside your head it was still; the clunky or obtuse parts fall out like so many bolts that weren't well fastened, and couldn't be detected until you started to speak." (I just had

some bolts drop from my mouth as I read a draft of this essay aloud.)
- Alter the way you physically experience your draft. Change the font (especially from a serif to a sans serif or vice versa), or scale down the size of the text and lay a chapter or the entire draft across the floor or hang it on a wall.
- Conjure up what W. H. Auden called the "Inner Censorate"—a group of specific readers whose reactions you value—and imagine their responses to the draft.

Bell also has excellent insights about how to achieve some of the subtler effects of fiction, especially foreshadowing and imagery. The editing process is where writers have the time and attention, after the initial intensity of creation, to add such niceties. As Bell puts it:

> It is said in feng shui, the ancient Chinese art of making space accommodate the spirit, that you should hang a picture or other tantalizing object on a wall at the end of a corridor that takes a turn. This is because the person walking down it should not face a blank space, but be pulled forth by an intriguing image; this way, she will make it to the end and turn. So it is with writing. Editing is the opportune time to get an overview of your story's proportions, rhythm and tension. When you reread your draft, look for the walls still left blank at the end of turning corridors, where you may place an arrow, as it were, to get your reader to make the turn.

Chapter endings are prime spots for foreshadowing.

Bell provides an illuminating analysis of F. Scott Fitzgerald's editing process for *The Great Gatsby* and also includes extended interviews with authors about the revision process. One of my favorites is with Ann Patchett, who offers up a wonderful baking metaphor: "I think of writing and editing in terms of folding, like you would fold in egg whites. You've got your egg whites beaten and you take a third of them and you lighten the batter by folding it in, and then you take a little bit and you fold it in, you fold it in—I don't feel like writing is linear as much as it is circular. There is this stirring movement of taking the story around in a circle, which means I am always writing back into it." That's the definition of revision as a creative act.

I'll leave you this week with a bit of wisdom from Bell: "To edit is to listen, above all; to hear past the emotional filters that distort the sound of our all too human words; and to then make choices rather than judgments." *Choices rather than judgments.* My role as an editor is to look for the missed opportunities—not in order to pass judgment on them, but in order to show a writer the choices open to them. You can do this for your work too. Approach your manuscript with an open mind and believe in its potential.

WEEK 13
AMONG THE WORD NERDS

It is week thirteen. I'm writing this essay on my long journey back to San Francisco from the American Copy Editors Society (ACES) conference in Providence, Rhode Island, an annual gathering of editors working in fields from journalism to healthcare to fiction. Rather than the usual book review this week, I'm going to discuss my favorite takeaways from the conference (aside from my Bananagrams tote bag):

- You know you are among word nerds when a speaker—in this case, Russell Harper, an editor of the *Chicago Manual of Style*—gets a laugh for an elaborate joke involving unicode characters, hexadecimals, and inverted commas.
- Authors, your words are in good hands. I spent three days in the company of 826 fellow editors who care deeply about your books, your words, and you. Many of them were listening intently as editors Tanya Gold and Christina Frey discussed how to phrase diplomatic author queries, how to

craft editorial letters that make authors feel like they are part of a conversation, and how to establish systems that help authors meet their goals.

- Introvert editors, this is the conference for you. I've never been to a conference full of self-aware introverts before, and I can tell you that it is a delight. If you need to be quiet, introverts will understand your cues and leave you be. If you are ready to socialize, introverts will understand all manner of awkwardness. (Plus, Bananagrams!)
- The English-language corpora hosted at Brigham Young University can answer many tricky editorial questions, particularly for historical fiction. Need to know whether "handbag" or "purse" was the prevalent term in the US in the 1920s? You can find an answer here—if you can learn how to navigate this hairy beast of a database. I'm grateful for some initial tips from Jonathan Owens.
- Most grammar and style rules can be broken—if you know the rules and know why you are breaking them, according to science fiction and fantasy copyeditor Richard Shealy (aka Shecky).
- When writing about death, try to avoid euphemisms (there are over three hundred in English!) and be aware of the diverse ways cultures discuss and mark death. In fiction, be sure that death isn't gratuitous and doesn't reinforce racial stereotypes, editor Sea Chapman advises.
- When you are writing or editing sex scenes, watch for continuity (are those pants already off?) and for extra appendages (characters are prone to sprout extra hands), copyeditor Sara Brady notes. For scenes with two or more participants, it can be

helpful to assign each character a different highlight color to check that pronouns and antecedents match up.
- The world is changing, we are changing, and language is changing. Makers of dictionaries and style guides are listening and weighing and discussing, and they make changes based on what they find in the world. As Peter Sokolowski, editor-at-large of *Merriam-Webster*, put it: "Progress does happen, things do change, and words do matter."

If you are interested in learning more about any of these topics, ACES hosts lists of previous conference sessions on their website, aceseditors.org.

WEEK 14

JESSICA BRODY, SAVE THE CAT! WRITES A NOVEL

It is week fourteen. How's the writing going? If you are stuck and need some creative solidarity, check out Camp NaNoWriMo. The main National Novel Writing Month is in November, but there are smaller programs in April and July. You'll find hundreds of other writers sprinting or stumbling along, trying to find their path.

I've been hearing buzz about Jessica Brody's *Save the Cat! Writes a Novel: The Last Book on Novel Writing You'll Ever Need* since it came out in 2018. While this is almost certainly not the last book on novel writing you'll ever need, I do think that you should have it in your collection. Like Shawn Coyne (in *Story Grid*, discussed in weeks seven and eight) and John Truby (in *The Anatomy of Story*, which I'll cover in week forty-five), Brody sets out to identify the key elements that all good stories have in common.

Brody breaks these elements down into fifteen "beats," following the methodology of Blake Snyder's advice for screenwriters. Brody, like Lisa Cron in *Wired for Story* (week four), zeroes in on the main character's transformation as the key to a strong plot. In her first chapter, she identifies the elements of transformation: (1) the hero's problem or flaw that needs to be fixed; (2) the want or goal the hero is pursuing; and (3) the hero's need, or the life lesson they need to learn. All great novels, Brody argues, "reprogram heroes. They transform human beings. And the beat sheet is essentially your reprogramming manual. It shows you which wires to cut, which code to alter, and in what order."

Brody notes that the most effective novels have both an external "A story" and an internal "B story." The fifteen beats, which she organizes into the traditional three-act structure, are the machine that powers the hero's transformation by weaving together the A and B stories. Brody explains each beat with admirable clarity, and her insights about the challenging second act are especially worth reading. Brody points out that the world of act two should be the "upside-down version" of the world of act one. Act two is when your hero tries to solve their problem in all the wrong ways, and it's also the point in the novel where you get to fulfill the "promise of the premise," showing your hero in the thick of the action. Brody lists a number of common ways you can raise the stakes for your hero at the midpoint of the novel and then shows you how to ride the momentum of the midpoint all the way into act three.

After outlining the fifteen beats, Brody devotes a long section of the book to discussing ten thematic genres (for example, "whydunit," "rites of passage," and "dude with a problem") and analyzing an example from each. These analyses are smart and thorough, and they show off the depth and breadth of Brody's reading. Doing a similar analysis for a popular book in your genre would be a useful exercise, either on your own or with a writers' group. I admire Brody for relying only on novels for her examples, especially since she is working with a methodology drawn from screenwriting. I can tell you from experience that it takes many hours of work (and generally two read-throughs of a novel) to do the kind of in-depth analysis she provides. But taking the time to read and study novels in a structured way like this can take you further than almost any other writing exercise I know.

At the end of the book, Brody spends some time discussing how both plotters and pantsers might use the beat structure, and she outlines her own method, which involves roughing out five key beats. But, she emphasizes, "Your beats are not carved in stone. Nor should they be." As you write you will encounter challenges and opportunities, just as you do in life, that will cause your plans to shift.

If you are concerned that following these fifteen beats will lead to formulaic writing, don't be. As Brody points out, there are no new stories under the sun. "Original is not an achievable goal in novel-writing. So just throw that word out the window right now. What is achievable is *fresh*." It doesn't take much shuffling to come up with a new way to tell the same story. Want proof? Go watch *Pretty in Pink* and then read Grady Hendrix's glorious '80s pastiche novel, *My Best Friend's Exorcism*, to see what I mean.

Only you can write your story, and *Save the Cat! Writes a Novel* might be the book that helps you unlock your plot.

WEEK 15
RENNI BROWNE AND DAVE KING, SELF-EDITING FOR FICTION WRITERS

It is week fifteen. This period of the year is always one of my most productive, and I've got a lot of exciting professional and creative projects lined up for the next two months before the distractions of summer set in. Maybe it's time for you to do a sprint too? What could you get done in the next eight weeks if you shuffle your schedule or your priorities?

This week's book—Renni Browne and Dave King's *Self-Editing for Fiction Writers: How to Edit Yourself into Print*—is one you'll want to turn to when you are ready to tackle the little details that make a novel sing. If you have an early draft and are still thinking about taking out a wall or changing the location of the kitchen or adding a sun-room off the back, you should skip ahead to week forty-seven and read my review of Sandra Scofield's *The Last Draft*, which will help you make these decisions. Browne and King's book is for when you are ready to think about whether cerulean blue is a brave choice for the kitchen walls or whether that old sofa will look right in the updated living room.

Browne and King cover all of the important topics you'll need to think through at this stage: how to balance showing and telling; how to describe your characters with subtlety and style; how to avoid common point-of-view pitfalls; and how to write dialogue, interior monologue, and action beats that sound natural. Their advice is clear and direct, supported by plentiful examples drawn from well-known writers and writing workshop participants. Each chapter closes with a checklist, as well as a few exercises. The exercises (for which the authors also provide an answer key) make this an ideal book to work through with a writing or critique group. As Browne and King point out, there are always multiple solutions to a given problem, and seeing how other writers clean up cluttered dialogue or a clunky sentence can teach you quite a lot.

Browne and King emphasize that writers should trust their readers—something beginning writers are often reluctant to do. As the authors put it: "Resist the Urge to Explain (R.U.E.)." Show your character being depressed or angry rather than explaining the emotion. Don't double-down and explain things that have already been shown through dialogue or action. Another reason to avoid repetition is that "when you try to accomplish the same effect twice, the weaker attempt is likely to undermine the power of the stronger one." This is an instance where "$1 + 1 = ½$." (Don't you love it when the rules of writing have the power to warp the rules of math?)

One of my favorite insights of the book is about the importance of interior monologue for novelists. As the authors note, "Movies and television may be influencing writers to write more visually, using immediate scenes with specific points of view to put their stories across." There's nothing wrong with visual, immediate scenes—but writers should use interior monologue, not just action, to capture the emotion of the scene: "On the page, readers can see how [a character] feels because they have the opportunity to move from action to thought and back again without ever being aware that anything out of the ordinary is happening. . . . One of the great gifts of literature is that it allows for the expression of unexpressed thoughts." An actor can convey inner emotion through facial expression, body language, or the way a dialogue line is said. Novelists can do the same thing more deeply and effectively using interior monologue and action tags, so don't neglect this powerful tool in your arsenal.

One big caveat about the advice here and in other writing craft books: Don't apply slash-and-burn editing techniques when you are revising. For example, after reading Browne and King's advice to avoid -ing constructions ("Pulling off her gloves, she turned to face him."), you might be tempted to pull up Word's search box and spend hours finding and eradicating every such construction in your novel. Don't do this! While you don't want to overuse this construction, you also don't want to litter your novel with sentences that awkwardly dance around it. As the authors themselves note, "If you see more than *one or two on a page*, start hunting around for alternatives" (emphasis mine).

I'd also encourage you to keep filling up your writer's brain with examples of what *to* do. Reading hones your writerly instincts and will give you confidence in your own choices. When you are reading, flag any sentence that makes you sit up and take notice. I frequently highlight passages on my Kindle to come back to later, and I also have a secret, antisocial Instagram account that I use to capture passages when I'm reading in print. An author's style might be very different from your own, but if you analyze their sentences to understand how they work their magic, you can often take away a lesson you can apply to your own writing. (For more on sentence modelling, jump ahead to my review of Virginia Tufte's *Artful Sentences* in week forty-six.)

Here's one I flagged recently in, of all places, a cookbook by Nigella Lawson called *How to Eat*: "Roast potatoes are another fraught area. I have, in the past, got frantic with despair as the time for the meat to be ready drew closer and the potatoes were still blond and untroubled in their roasting pan." Nigella's charming Britishisms mightn't be suitable for your style, but you can try out her technique of transferring adjectives from one realm to another. We expect to find adjectives like "blond and untroubled" applied to children, and so to see them applied to potatoes wakes us right up—and injects a note of dark humor given that these innocent potatoes are being roasted and eaten. Are we reading a cookbook or a Grimms' fairy tale?

You could wander into a bookstore this afternoon with a notebook and pen to start your own collection of model sentences and call it work.

WEEK 16
CHUCK WENDIG, DAMN FINE STORY

It is week sixteen. How's the writing going? My work has mostly been on hold this week as I played tour guide for visiting family. It was a giddy highlights reel of sights and sounds and tastes. But the image that sticks with me is one that I stored away at the very beginning of the week.

The San Francisco Museum of Modern Art is one of my favorite places in the city, and the Alexander Calder gallery has been one of my favorite spots in the museum since it reopened a few years ago. The gallery has been rearranged since I was last there, and I was immediately drawn to a stark white mobile placed against a wall the color of lapis lazuli.[1] Like all of Calder's work, this mobile, titled *Moths II*, plays with balance, with a few larger shapes on the right side providing ballast for the string of smaller shapes that trail off to the left. The shapes move gently when they are caught in the air currents coming from the gallery doors leading outside, but the curved horizontal axis keeps the piece strong and steady.

I thought of Calder's mobile often this week as I read Chuck Wendig's *Damn Fine Story: Mastering the Tools of a*

Powerful Narrative because it makes a perfect visual metaphor for Wendig's primary advice, which is to find the spine of your story and then experiment until you achieve balance. I can imagine Calder playing around with his shapes, moving them along the curved spine, seeing just how far out he could extend them without destroying the balance of the piece.

Wendig, similarly, wants you to dive into your characters and setting and ask questions and mess around with answers until you find the shape of your story. He has much advice to give and even some rules to convey, but his overriding message is that there is no formula: "This isn't science. This isn't math. You can't plug a bunch of narrative components into an equation and spit out a perfect story. The truth is, most of what I'm telling you here is wildly imperfect. It's guesswork. It's lies layered with horseshit layered with I-don't-know-what-I'm-talking-about. You don't have the answers, either." But Wendig knows a good story when he sees it. More importantly, he believes that you know how to spot one too.

Like Lisa Cron, whose book we covered in week four, Wendig believes that characters should fuel the plot rather than vice versa: "We have this idea of plot as a big, explosive thing. A galaxy in strife! A world in danger! Hidden treasure! Secret weapon! . . . . When storytellers have an exterior framework into which they then plug the characters, the characters operate as secondary, as afterthoughts. And the audience has no one to ground them in the story. Characters are everything. Characters drive the narrative." This is true, Wendig argues, because "the small story"—the emotional throughline, the story about "characters and their personal drama"—matters more to us than the big story. We may think we are there for the fireworks, but we're really there for the deep truths.

My favorite insight of the book is that every character in

a novel "shares the same narrative oxygen," and each one—supporting characters and antagonists included—is the protagonist of their own story. Some characters in a story are on parallel paths, moving in the same direction. These characters are often allies, or become allies. Other characters are following paths that are perpendicular to one another. It's at these intersections where paths cross that the plot really occurs. Think about the possibilities here: Two (or more) characters can meet and clash, and then move on past one another, continuing their separate journeys. An intersection could become a T-junction, a place where one character's path ends or where a character joins the path of another.

As Wendig points out, seeing every single character as the hero of their own story will automatically steer you away from missteps like creating "strong female characters" whose sole purpose is to "leverage the dudes into action." Instead, give all of your characters agency. "Let them all have problems, solutions, wants, and fears, and let them act on those things as independent architects within the narrative." Readers don't need a lot of background about the problems and goals of minor characters, but just a few details can show the tip of the iceberg and cue readers that there is much more below the surface.

While Wendig deliberately avoids providing a grand theory of story or a set formula for creating a successful one, the book is packed with valuable material, delivered with a great deal of wit and some top-shelf cursing. Wendig's annotated list of "twists, tweaks, and tickles" you can use to juice up your plot will be helpful for anyone stuck in the "long slog of the mushy middle," and his list of elements every scene needs to have would be a perfect checklist for a writer doing an initial revision pass on their first draft. He writes accessibly and practically about abstract concepts like theme, trope, and metaphor, and his advice about transitions is the best I've seen. (In a nutshell: use them only when absolutely necessary; when they are necessary, make them do double-duty—turn them into proper scenes that "further the story by deepening a character's arc, giving us insight into the character, driving home the story's theme, or revealing a crucial piece of information.")

Wendig admits that, even with dozens of successful titles under his belt, he still sometimes suffers from imposter syndrome. He combats it with a profound belief that storytelling is for all of us. "Storytelling is a shared tradition," he declares. "We all get to pass around the talking stick and the magic witch's eye. It's not just for the priests or the chosen few." So dive into that deep well of stories inside you and see what you're able to bring to the surface. Experiment with the pieces, rework that all-important narrative spine until you find balance, and then grab the talking stick and tell your story to the audience waiting around the fire for another tale.

WEEK 17
CONSTANCE HALE, SIN AND SYNTAX

It is week seventeen. Reviewing my calendar, I see that I've worked on ten different books this week, doing everything from intensive developmental editing to simple cheerleading. I love this work, and I will always be an editor first and a writer second. But I've come to treasure the hours I spend writing these essays, when I, too, get to face the freedom and the terror of the blank page.

This week's book is the wonderfully titled *Sin and Syntax: How to Craft Wicked Good Prose* by Constance Hale. I realized this week while reading it that I have been unconsciously searching this year for The One Book to Rule Them All. Or perhaps two: one on narrative structure and another on sentence-level writing. Looking at Hale's table of contents—which takes us from "Words" (nouns, adverbs, conjunctions, and so on) to "Sentences" (subjects and predicates, phrases and clauses) to "Music" (melody, rhythm, voice)—I thought this book could perhaps be The One.

Readers, *Sin and Syntax* is not The One. But I suspect that there is no such thing as The One. Once I put aside my desire for a magical unicorn that clearly explains the confusing morass that is English grammar *and* provides astute and illuminating advice on slippery matters of style, all in one manageable package, I found a lot to like in Hale's book.

Each chapter is organized into four sections: bones (grammar principles), flesh (writing lessons), cardinal sins (errors to avoid), and carnal pleasures (examples of good writing and suggestions for how to play with rules). This structure leads to some repetition across sections, but it also allows Hale to show readers just how flexible—and exciting—the English language is.

Hale's best advice is in the "Word" section, where she challenges writers to think about both the denotation (the literal meaning) and the connotations (the implicit meanings) of every word, as well as "its sensuousness: its sound, its cadence, its spirit." For Hale, choosing a word entails exploring its various layers:

> First, it must precisely render an image: pick bungalow if you're describing a one-story house with a low-pitched roof. Second, your noun must be evocative, its connotations conjuring a realm of emotion or sensation: stay with bungalow (or perhaps choose cottage) if you're capturing coziness, a homey atmosphere. Finally, your noun must be apt—its associations, its links to other words and ideas, must complement your meaning. Are the occupants a bunch of frat boys? Then crash pad might work better.

Hale reminds us that the stronger the word, the more room it needs in a sentence. Stripping off extraneous adjectives or replacing an adverb + weak verb combination with a single powerful verb can improve your sentences. As Hale puts it, "Many adverbs—especially the how? variety—merely prop up a limp verb. Strike 'speaks softly' and insert whispers. Erase 'eats hungrily' in favor of devours."

In her "Sentence" section, Hale offers the best conceptual explanation I've read of how the parts of a sentence work together. As Hale explains it, every sentence is like a mini-narrative, a story: "A sentence needs a What (the subject) and a So What (the predicate). The subject is the person, place, thing, or idea we want to express something about; the predicate expresses the action, condition, or effect of that subject. The predicate expresses a predicament—the situation the subject is in." For a sentence to tell its story effectively, both of these parts must be clear and vivid.

"Relish every word" appears as a section header three different times in the book, and it is one of Hale's "five new principles of prose." (The others are "aim deep but be simple"; "take risks"; "seek beauty"; and "find the right pitch.") Along with your sentence collection, which I discussed in week fifteen, you might start a word collection for yourself, noting words with special connections to a subject or character, or words that are especially allusive. The online dictionary Wordnik.com is a compendium of definitions, etymologies, and examples that allows you to maintain a list of favorites or even adopt a word. I've adopted *smite*, which I love for its Anglo-Saxon bite. Underneath the seemingly harmless fluff of *smitten* lies a verb that also means *to destroy*, *to blast*, and *to afflict*.

I'll remind you again: this word-focused attention is the province of revision, not of drafting. If you stop to consider all of these aspects of every word before you commit it to paper, I guarantee you will be frustrated and stuck. And likely wordless. But once you've filled up your blank page with words and you've got your story structure set, *Sin and Syntax* will help you cook up sentences that readers will devour.

WEEK 18

JANE SMILEY, 13 WAYS OF LOOKING AT THE NOVEL

It is week eighteen. How's the writing going for you? If you are feeling dull or jaded, this week's book might be the antidote, so let's get right into it.

Jane Smiley's *13 Ways of Looking at the Novel* is not, as far as I can tell, very much read. I haven't come across it once in all the lists of recommended books for writers I have scanned while planning this year of reading. Yet Jane Smiley is a well-regarded novelist. *A Thousand Acres* won the Pulitzer in 1992, and she has written in a remarkable range of genres, from historical fiction to mysteries to comedies of manners.

The truth is, *13 Ways of Looking at the Novel* is a big, unwieldy book that resists categorization. Smiley does not, as the title implies, present us with thirteen well-defined lenses for exploring the novel as a genre. Instead, her chapters tackle big questions: What *is* a novel? How did it develop across centuries? How do novels interact with history, morality, psychology, and politics? How do you write one yourself? What happens when a novelist gets stuck? What does someone learn when she reads one hundred novels over the course of three years?

There *are* thirteen chapters (including the introduction) in the main section of the book, and I imagine Smiley's editorial team throwing up their hands in a meeting and declaring, "Let's just call the thing *13 Ways of Looking at the Novel*." It's a wandering, questioning, circuitous kind of book. There are no section headers, no bullet points, no checklists. You have to find your own path through it and make your own meaning from it.

In the early chapters, Smiley starts from first principles. When she asks "What is a novel?" her first move is to consider the book as an object: "An inexpensive paperback book from a reputable publisher is a small, rectangular, boxlike object a few inches long, a few inches wide, and an inch or so thick. It is easy to stack and store, easy to buy, keep, give away, or throw away. As an object, it is user-friendly and routine, a mature technological form, hard to improve upon and easy to like. Many people, myself among them, feel better at the mere sight of a book."

Slowly, Smiley builds toward a bigger point: "The leaves of paper pressed together are reserved and efficient as well as cool and dry. They protect each other from damage. They take up little space. Spread open, they offer some information, but they don't offer too much, and they don't force it upon me or anyone else. They invite perusal. Underneath the open leaves, on either side, are hidden ones that have been read or remain to be read. The reader may or may not experience them. The choice is always her own."

Smiley returns often to the concepts of power, freedom, and choice. She compares novels to a meditation guided by the writer and to a game in which the writer sets the rules. Always, the reader has a choice about whether or not to participate in the meditation or the game. And, as Smiley notes, it's a choice the reader must make over and over again, over the course of days or weeks: "While all art forms promote this state of receptivity, with the novel it is uniquely sustained—it is not possible, for example, to contemplate a painting for ten or twelve hours, the amount of time the average reader would need to read a five-hundred-page novel."

The prosaic quality of length, then, turns out to be a key feature of novels and a source of their power. Smiley observes, "When I have read a long novel, when I have entered systematically into a sensibility that is alien to mine, the author's or a character's, when I have become interested in another person because he is interesting, not because he is privileged or great, there is a possibility that at the end I will be a degree less self-centered than I was at the beginning, that I will be a degree more able to see the world as another sees it." As a result, novels have the potential to be a subversive force in the world.

These are big claims, and Smiley uses formal, almost academic language to make them. But chapter 10, "A Novel of Your Own (I)," marks a dramatic change in tone and tense. Instead of "the reader" or "the novelist," there is, simply, "you": "Now that you have decided to begin your novel, you may congratulate yourself. You have not been asked or groomed to write a novel. . . . Chances are, no one wants you to write your novel—if they say they do, they are just meaning that you should get it over with or get on with it. . . . You are, therefore, free." Just like the reader, the writer has the power to continue or to stop. "Remembering at all times that no one ever asked you to write that novel, you will at least be preserved from feeling victimized by your work," Smiley counsels.

In this chapter and the next, Smiley lays out her advice about such familiar matters as plot, characters, and point of view in terms that are clear and encouraging. My favorite insight is about the relationship between setting and theme:

"As with character and action, setting and theme feed one another. If your themes are too general, then investigate your setting more closely, and anchor your characters more deeply within their circumstances. If your story seems too trivial, then ask yourself about the connections between these circumstances and the larger human condition."

Smiley also provides sound practical advice on the writing process. The first step is to write a rough draft without getting mired down. "Every rough draft," Smiley counsels, "by being complete, is perfect." Smiley then advises examining the exposition (the beginning 10 percent or so), the rising action or middle, and the climax, taking notes about what's working and what's not working. She reassures writers, "You have plenty of ingenuity. If you are receptive to your rough draft but detached from it, you will come up with some sort of method that will make your novel palpable to you and spur your inspiration with a sense of progress."

13 Ways can also be read as a story itself—the story of a writer finding her way back to her words. Smiley tells us in the introduction that the idea for this book emerged when she became stuck two-thirds of the way through the first draft of her 2001 novel *Good Faith*: "I felt like Dante's narrator at the beginning of *The Divine Comedy*. I had wandered into a dark wood. I didn't know the way out. I was afraid." Smiley leaves that story open and doesn't return to it until chapter 12 when she describes how she found her way out of the wood. Along the way, however, we can also see her falling in love with Boccaccio's *Decameron*, which would become the inspiration for *Ten Days in the Hills*, the novel she wrote after *Good Faith*. Her reading, in other words, allowed her not just to finish one book but also to find the seed of her next. (I haven't read *Ten Days in the Hills*, but Smiley's description of what the book felt like to her in its early days makes me want to: "The new book looks spherical and self-contained, but jammed with things, like a spaceship made of Venetian glass, shining, intricate, and full of colors, not like any novel ever looked to me before.")

13 Ways also offers the pleasure of vicariously comparing notes with a thoughtful, intelligent reader on books you know and love. (Or hate, as the case may be; Smiley, for example, dislikes Henry James's "domineering manner" and finds the style of John Steinbeck's *The Grapes of Wrath* "cloying.") The second half of the book is composed of mini-essays on the hundred novels she read. Smiley suggests "that it be used like an old trunk full of fabric samples or a box of costume jewelry—it is not to be read through from beginning to end in search of a cohesive argument, but to be rummaged about in, in search of something interesting or striking." Smiley shares my fascination with *The Heptaméron*, the sixteenth-century story cycle written by the French queen Marguerite de Navarre, calling it "a kind of rough draft for many novels yet to be written." And I love her assessment of Anthony Trollope, who deserves to be more widely read today: "Trollope doesn't mind a little sin, and he knows that lives go on after the plot ends.... He is a novelist for adults." Indeed.

13 Ways of Looking at the Novel also offers a model for a program of active, engaged reading that could become a daily practice or an intensive period of study for times in which you are stuck. I imagine a reader's version of Julia Cameron's morning pages (a practice of freewriting first thing in the morning, popular among writers): Choose a novel to study, preferably one that is outside of your typical range of reading, read a few pages every morning, and try to pick apart how it works.[1] How do these specific sets of words work together to create meaning? What effects are these words having on you, the reader? How does the author achieve these effects? This is active, pencil-in-hand reading.

"For inspiration, keep reading novels," Smiley tells us. "As you aim for perfection, don't forget that there is no perfect novel, that because every novel is built out of specifics, every novel offers some pleasures but does not offer some others, and while you can try to achieve as many pleasures as possible, some cancel out others."

13 Ways of Looking at the Novel is the book to turn to when you find yourself wondering why you are spending so much time and intellectual energy on this novel-writing business. Smiley points out that "at the base of every novel is an argument the author is making about why a novel is worth writing, selling, and reading." To read one, then, is to be reassured that this game you are playing, this extended meditation you are creating, is important. As Smiley puts it, "It's worth knowing that serious thoughts are being thought, and also that serious fun is being made of fools everywhere. It's also worth knowing, in dangerous times, that dangers have come and gone and we still have these books." We need to have your book among them.

WEEK 19
TWYLA THARP, THE CREATIVE HABIT

It is week nineteen. I can just see my two-week summer road trip starting to appear over the horizon, which is helping me focus on what I want to accomplish before that big juicy break. If you know you have a vacation coming up, try to do a mini-sprint leading up to it—you'll enjoy your break even more knowing that you have made the most of the time before it.

This week's book is *The Creative Habit: Learn It and Use It for Life*, by Twyla Tharp and Mark Reiter. (Because the narrative "I" in the book is clearly Tharp's, I'll be attributing the ideas to her in this piece.) As a choreographer, Tharp's work only comes to life if she can communicate her ideas to her dancers, and those finely honed directorial skills come through in *The Creative Habit*. Tharp's voice is sharp, fierce, and honest. This is a woman who has developed the self-described "steeliness of character" and creative confidence to audition nine hundred dancers in order to hire four—in other words, to say *no* to 896 people.

If you read Elizabeth Gilbert's *Big Magic*, you may remember her metaphor for handling her fears: fear is allowed to come on the figurative road trip she is taking with creativity, but it's never allowed to drive the car. Here's the image Tharp reaches for: "In those long and sleepless nights when I'm unable to shake my fears sufficiently, I borrow a biblical epigraph from Dostoyevsky's *The Demons*: I see my fears being cast into the bodies of wild boars and hogs, and I watch them rush to a cliff where they fall to their deaths." If *Big Magic* is a cocktail, *The Creative Habit* is a shot of whisky, neat. You'll know which you need. Here's another sip: Worried that some other artist has already created the work you want to make? "Honey, it's all been done before. Nothing's really original. Not Homer or Shakespeare and certainly not you. Get over yourself." Got it? And one more: "If you're at a dead end, take a deep breath, stamp your foot, and shout 'Begin!' You never know where it will take you."

Tharp's courage and confidence come in part from the fact that she works in the high-stakes crucible of choreography. For a moment, imagine that instead of facing a blank page or a blank screen, you walk into a white room, knowing that in five weeks you will be staging a dance that you haven't yet choreographed:

> My dancers expect me to deliver because my choreography represents their livelihood. The presenters in Los Angeles expect the same because they've sold a lot of tickets to people with the promise that they'll see something new and interesting from me. The theater owner (without really thinking about it) expects it as well; if I don't show up, his theater will be empty for a week. That's a lot of people, many of whom I've never met, counting on me to be creative. But right now I'm not thinking about any of this. I'm in a room with the obligation to create a major dance piece. The dancers will be here in a few minutes. What are we going to do?

Remember this scenario the next time you have writer's block, and feel lucky that your stakes are not quite so high.

Alongside the straight talk, Tharp offers inventive exercises designed to work your creative muscles. For example, write an autobiography to uncover your creative DNA; observe a man and woman together, write down twenty actions they perform, and then create a story about them; mine an old photograph from your childhood for memories; drop a pile of coins on a table and rearrange them in a pleasing pattern; write down a list of twenty questions you want to know about a topic you plan to write on; physically act out a verb, like you are playing solitaire charades. One that's particularly well-suited for writers: develop what Tharp calls your "metaphor quotient" by searching for figures in clouds, studying the linguistic roots of words, or connecting two seemingly unrelated works of art. "Metaphor," Tharp says, "is the lifeblood of all art, if it is not art itself. Metaphor is our vocabulary for connecting what we're experiencing now with what we have experienced before. It's not only how we express what we remember, it's how we interpret it—for ourselves and others." These connections and interpretations are what make your work fresh, even if it can never be wholly original.

Tharp has the experience and wisdom to understand her own creative process and put it into words, something many artists, even writers, never achieve. She calls her initial explorations "scratching": "It's like clawing at the side of a mountain to get a toehold, a grip, some sort of traction to keep moving upward and onward." Scratching can be reading, listening, improvising with an open mind and energetic spirit. "Scratching is real and tangible. It bloodies your fingernails," Tharp says.

After scratching comes planning, but overplanning can cripple your creativity: "Too much planning implies you've got it all under control. That's boring, unrealistic, and dangerous. It lulls you into a complacency that removes one of the artist's most valuable conditions: being pissed. Art is competitive with yourself, with the past, with the future. It is a special war zone where first you make the rules, and then you test the consequences." The only goal in the planning stage is to identify the spine for your work—the core idea that will guide your intentions and creativity.

Tharp also has wise things to say about the ebbs and flows of creativity—what she calls "ruts" and "grooves"—and she has the most thorough, insightful discussion of the power of failure I've seen in any book on creativity. "Every creative person has to learn to deal with failure," Tharp says, "because failure, like death and taxes, is inescapable. If Leonardo and Beethoven and Goethe failed on occasion, what makes you think you'll be the exception?" Private failure teaches you to edit out bad ideas, exercise your judgment, and set higher and higher expectations for yourself. And when you do fail in public, "you are forcing yourself to learn a whole new set of skills, skills that have nothing to do with creating and everything to do with surviving." This is how you become a stronger human, allowing you to take even bigger risks and achieve greater heights in your creativity.

Above all, Tharp will remind you again and again in *The Creative Habit* that it is all worth it. The bloody scratching, those fear pigs falling to their deaths, the private ruts, and the public failures—they eventually lead to magic. "When it all comes together," she tells us, "a creative life has the nourishing power we normally associate with food, love, and faith. . . . It permits me to walk into a white room and walk out dancing." Tuck that metaphor away in your mind and let it do its work. One day soon, I want to see you walk into that white room of the blank page and walk out dancing.

WEEK 20
JANET BURROWAY, WRITING FICTION

It is week twenty. How's the writing coming? In my world, it's been a week of cold rain and sick kids and disrupted schedules. A stale, shut-in feeling has been threatening to close in all week, but I've managed to keep it at bay by focusing on stories.

I wrapped up copyedits on a short story with a deliciously unreliable narrator and a wicked twist at the end, and I started a developmental edit of a promising historical novel that has given me the excuse to reread *A Midwife's Tale*, Laurel Thatcher Ulrich's Pulitzer Prize–winning biography of an eighteenth-century American midwife. Reading about the intrepid Martha Ballard walking across the frozen Kennebec River on the way to a delivery, falling through the ice, pulling herself out, and borrowing a neighbor's horse to get to her patient was just what I needed to pull myself out of my own self-pitying funk.

Perhaps it was the funk, but I found this week's book, Janet Burroway's *Writing Fiction: A Guide to Narrative Craft*, uncongenial. I respect it and trust much of its wisdom—but I did not *like* it. I spent a lot of time this week mulling over why, and I'll circle back to that at the end of this essay, but let's start with the nuggets of wisdom I excavated.

Burroway excels at clearly and thoroughly explaining the key principles of fiction writing and finding (or creating) examples that illustrate the principle at work. She identifies three kinds of dialogue (direct, indirect, summarized) and three uses for it (to reveal character, set a mood, move the action). Similarly, she outlines four direct ways to present character ("appearance, speech, action, and thought") and two indirect ways ("authorial interpretation and presentation by another character") and advises on why you would choose one method over another. Her discussion of point of view is organized around these questions: "Who speaks? To whom? In what form? At what distance from the action?" She presents the available options and shows the effects each one can have.

I particularly liked Burroway's discussion of summary and scene, which she likens to the "mortar" and the "building blocks" of the story. Many beginning writers excel at scene but struggle with summary, in part because they don't understand how to manipulate it. Burroway provides a helpful distinction between sequential and circumstantial summary. Sequential summary compresses a specific period of time, as Margaret Atwood does in this passage from *Lady Oracle*:

> The snow finally changed to slush and then to water, which trickled down the hill of the bridge in two rivulets, one on either side of the path; the path itself turned to mud. The bridge was damp, it smelled rotten, the willow branches turned yellow, the skipping ropes came out.

Atwood is showing us the familiar transformation from winter to spring, but her use of specific details in this summary ground the reader more deeply in her setting and her story.

Circumstantial summary, on the other hand, helps writers generalize, setting the stage for the moment when events do not follow the usual pattern. Compare, for example, another passage from *Lady Oracle*:

> My own job was fairly simple. I stood at the back of the archery range, wearing a red leather apron, and rented out the arrows. When the barrels of arrows were almost used up, I'd go down to the straw targets. . . . The difficulty was that we couldn't make sure all the arrows had actually been shot before we went to clear the targets. Rob would shout, 'Bows DOWN, please, arrows OFF the string,' but occasionally someone would let an arrow go, on purpose or by accident. This was how I got shot. We'd pulled the arrows and the men were carrying the barrels back to the line; I was replacing a target face, and I'd just bent over.

The change in verb mood signals the shift from summary to scene. The usual is marked by the conditional *would*: "I would go down," "Rob would shout." The shift to scene happens in the deliberately compressed sentence "This was how I got shot," which uses the indicative *was*. Atwood then uses past perfect tense ("He had pulled . . . I'd just bent") to rewind slightly to explain the scene. The purpose of both kinds of summary is to give readers the information they need in order to understand the significance of the scene you are going to show (that arrow in the narrator's ass), and to do so artfully, weaving in hints about character or setting or theme.

I also admired Burroway's insistence that fiction is driven not just by conflict, but by "a pattern of connection and disconnection between characters that is the main source of its emotional effect." It's the emotional effect, Burroway argues, that is the true power of a work like *Romeo and Juliet*, the element that "makes the otherwise trivial tale of a feud into a tragedy."

And this point also explains, I think, why I found *Writing Fiction* difficult to like. Even though Burroway, a novelist herself, refers occasionally to her own writing practices and experiences, she's hard to locate in the book. *Writing Fiction* was first published in 1982; the tenth edition was published in early 2019. While much has been gained in this update (Burroway and her coauthors draw examples from an enjoyably fresh and diverse group of authors), I wonder if Burroway's distinctive voice and perspective have been lost. References to Ultrasuede jackets and telephone books sit uneasily alongside references to Snapchat. The former feel unmoored, left behind, while the latter feel obligatory, a calculated reference point for an assumed audience of college students.

The original story of the book (nonfiction books have stories too) has been disrupted, and it hasn't been replaced with a new narrative through-thread. Burroway, like myself and probably many of you, has lived in the Age of Ultrasuede and in the Age of Snapchat. What has changed about stories and storytelling and the teaching of storytelling in that time? Burroway reaches for an answer in the introduction—"We are, I believe, at a point in history where, the computer and the internet having reintroduced writing as a constant activity, the elite again becomes the demotic, with both good and bad consequences"—but the writing here is stilted, overly formal, and noncommittal. She recognizes the influence of visual media like film and television on the novel, pointing out that while nineteenth-century readers were carefully shepherded from point A to point B by a solicitous, often chatty, omniscient narrator, twenty-first-century readers don't even blink when asked to walk from the deep point of view of character A to the deep point of view of character B across the narrow little bridge of a blank line or perhaps an asterisk or two.

And yet Burroway largely portrays film, television, and genre fiction as an army of barbarians storming the cloister of literary fiction: "The tendency of recent literature is to move away from rigid categories, toward a loosening or crossing of story types—so-called genre-busting or genre-bending, in which genre fiction presses at the bounds of literary fiction." Genre fiction is variously described as plot driven, unrealistically and unreasonably optimistic about the inherent fairness of life, and written to appeal to a narrow range of interests—it's positioned as the marker that writers should be steering away from and not toward. I think Burroway may be misreading the waters here and that we are already at a point where the barrier between literary fiction and genre fiction is starting to crumble. (See, for example, Marlon James's remarks on episode 17 of the *Fiction/Non/Fiction* podcast.)[1] Once you begin to see literary fiction as simply another type of story, with its own conventions and reader expectations, it's hard to go back to the ranked dichotomy.

Burroway tells us that "creative writing must remain a college subject because, like philosophy and history (and similarly unremunerative studies), it is neither taught nor learned without pedagogical effort." *Writing Fiction* has the feel of obligation clinging to it—the whiff of assigned reading and compulsory writing and joyless grading. Compare this vision to that of Chuck Wendig in *Damn Fine Story* (week sixteen), who talks about "story," not about "fiction," and who, notably, writes everything from comic books to RPGs to novels:

Telling stories is a powerful common denominator. And listening to stories is as vital and as common as breathing. We are bound together by our stories. We share traits and tales through those narratives—and we also help to spread empathy and compassion and critical thinking through them. Stories are the ripples that carry water from my shore to yours, and yours back to mine.

I love classrooms. I spent decades in them, long after I had to, both as a student and as a teacher. Classrooms can be the best place to question fundamental assumptions and break down barriers and experiment. But I think that, right now, I want to be at the campfire passing the talking stick, telling my story and listening to other people tell theirs and figuring out how they all work and what new ways of telling might emerge.

WEEK 21

JAMES FREY, HOW TO WRITE A DAMN GOOD MYSTERY

It is week twenty-one. A dear friend summoned the courage this week to show me a piece of writing that is trying to become something. She's not sure exactly what kind of story she is telling or even who the narrator is yet, but I could see the promise—the authentic emotion, some vivid turns of phrase—shimmering behind the words. I told her to keep going, and that's what I say to you too. Keep writing. Find the time, find the energy, find the words. See your story through.

Now, on to this week's book, *How to Write a Damn Good Mystery* by James N. Frey. (This James Frey is the Edgar-nominated mystery writer, not the author of the controversial memoir *A Million Little Pieces*.) To be completely honest, I picked this book because I was curious to see whether Frey addressed the literary fiction–genre fiction dichotomy I saw in Janet Burroway's *Writing Fiction*, which I reviewed last week.

It didn't take me long to find it. In chapter 2, Frey discusses throwing out the "dumbos" who show up in his mystery-writing classes because they've failed at writing literary fiction and want to try something they think is easier. "Most alleged literary novels," Frey instructs us, "aren't even novels at all, because they don't tell a story. What they do is depress the reader for, oh, about three hundred pages, then the writer mercifully kills off the main character at the end. This proves what? Life sucks, then you die. How very dreary." Okay, then.

My hunch is that Burroway hasn't read much genre fiction and Frey hasn't read much literary fiction. I'd urge you not to make the same mistake. As Jane Smiley reminded us in *13 Ways of Looking at the Novel* (week eighteen), the job of every novelist is "to develop a theory of how it feels to be alive." Romance writers and thriller writers and literary fiction writers are all pursuing this same goal. Take a look and see what you can learn from them. Read everything. And then follow this advice from Frey: "Write what you like to read." I think Burroway would agree.

Let's move on to what Frey has to tell us about writing a novel. His advice is different in tone and structure from Burroway's, but they agree about the fundamental building blocks of good fiction. Like Burroway, Frey discusses how to create compelling characters, how to build a sound plot, how to shape a dynamic scene, and how to write good prose. On this last point, Frey reminds us to use not just all five senses (sight, smell, sound, touch, taste) but also our characters' sixth "psychic" sense—their intuitions about other characters. This is especially true for mysteries and thrillers, where the solution to the crime or the satisfying last-minute rescue often hinges on the instincts of the sleuth or the quick reaction of the hero. But I think it holds true for other genres as well. Often your protagonist is the protagonist because they have sharper psychological instincts than your other characters and, thus, the power to share their insights with the reader.

Frey is firmly in the plotting camp, disliking the "reams of pages that eventually go into the recycle bin" that is the frequent result of the pantsing method. In place of what a pantser might call an exploratory draft, Frey recommends writing complete biographies of major characters (including their physiology, sociology, and psychology), as well as writing journal entries from their points of view in order to further define their personalities, motives, and voices. (Presumably, most of this material is also destined for the recycle bin, but we won't quibble.)

Once you have worked through all of these preliminaries, you are ready to begin plotting. For mysteries, Frey makes the excellent point that it is the murderer who is the "author of the plot behind the plot" and that it is the murderer's motive that is the engine of the novel. He starts by writing out a summary of that plot, working out why and how the murder was committed, before starting his "stepsheet," which is like a step-by-step breakdown of the plot. For mysteries, Frey advises creating separate sections that follow what the reader will see and what is happening "off-stage," in order to keep all of the pieces straight.

Frey walks us through a five-act plot structure that mirrors the stages of the classic hero's journey:

- Act I: Tells How the Hero/Detective Accepts the Mission to Find the Murderer
- Act II: Tells How the Hero/Detective Is Tested and Changes, and, in the Pivotal Scene, Dies and Is Reborn
- Act III: Tells How the Hero/Detective Is Tested Again and Finally Succeeds

- Act IV: Tells How the Hero/Detective Traps the Murderer
- Act V: Tells How the Events of the Story Impact the Major Characters

Frey believes that if you have taken the time to create complex characters whose psychology and motivations you understand, you can simply drop them into the plot and let them create the story: "Let your characters do the work. Think of what they will do, what they want, what is clever and resourceful for them to do, and if you have created dynamic characters, you will have a dynamic plot."

My favorite aspect of *Damn Good Mystery* is that we get to see Frey do just this. He creates a mystery plot from scratch, starting from the seed of an idea about a setting in Montana. We see him create his characters, refine and expand and fine-tune them, and then we see him work through his stepsheet, act by act, with his notes about why he is making certain choices. Similarly, we get to see him in the act of revision, showing us progressive versions of scenes.

Remember Burroway's helpful advice last week about using sequential and circumstantial summary? Frey makes a related point about the difference between summary and dramatic narrative:

> **Summary:** Shakti spent the afternoon knocking on doors all up and down Main Street, asking everyone she met if they knew a man named Swift. No one admitted that they did. By evening, she was tired, and went back to her hotel and prayed and meditated till past nine, then went to bed.
>
> **Dramatic narrative:** Shakti began canvassing the town, desperate to find this "Swifty" person. About noon, just as

> there was a break in the snowstorm, the sun burst through the clouds, making North of Nowhere sparkle under a heavy blanket of snow. Shakti worked her way north, stopping first at the hardware store and asking the moon-faced clerk, who shook his head blankly, and an old ranchhand with a corncob pipe, who said he never did hear of the man, and a man with dark features wearing a hunting jacket, who told her to leave town. She covered the west side of Main and started back, her feet frozen in her unlined boots. More clouds were moving into the valley in the afternoon—dark clouds, meaning there'd be more snow by morning...

The dramatic narrative version puts readers into the scene, providing sensory details that fill out the setting, cue a mood, and reveal the psychology of major and minor characters. Frey also demonstrates how to work a tiny piece of a scene—a snippet of dialogue or a quick action sequence—into the midst of a dramatic narrative, an advanced technique that can help you cover a lot of ground in your plot while keeping readers engaged.

Frey also suggests a writing exercise that might be useful for those of you who are still scratching around an idea. He suggests literally typing out, word for word, a scene from the work of a writer whose prose you admire. Then write a similar scene, trying to capture the same style. Keep doing this, imitating various styles and voices, Frey says, and "you'll soon discover that your own, individual, distinctive styles will emerge, styles suited to your personality and to the particular story you are writing, styles unlike any of the styles you've been imitating."

Why not try out one of Frey's writing exercises? How about today? How about right now? Draft a character bio or a little scene in a note-taking app on your phone. Go out on the front steps or the back porch or to a bench in the park with a notebook and a beverage (perhaps a Bitter White Lady cocktail: gin, lemon juice, honey, bitters, and egg white shaken over ice, served in a coupe glass with a grapefruit zest twist) and see what happens.

WEEK 22
JANICE HARDY, REVISING YOUR NOVEL

It is week twenty-two. I'm writing this essay while trying to block out the sound of the leaf blower being wielded next door (puzzling, since we are more of a taco truck kind of neighborhood than a leaf blower kind of neighborhood), which is a fair metaphor for the kind of week I've had. Sometimes it takes a great deal of effort to block out the external or internal noise. Recognize the draw on your energy, and then try to keep going anyway. Maybe the week's work will have to be heavily revised somewhere down the line (you'll encounter it again and remember, "Oh yeah, that was the leaf blower week."), but if you can keep the words flowing, even at a trickle, that's better than stopping altogether because it requires exponentially more effort and willpower to start back up.

Now, on to this week's book, *Revising Your Novel: First Draft to Finished Draft*, by Janice Hardy. Some books about revision are contemplative or even lyrical (Susan Bell's *Artful Edit*, which I reviewed in week twelve, comes to mind). Hardy's book is on the other side of the spectrum, focused on practical steps that will help an author analyze their work and fix the flaws. There are a lot of energizing *now*s and *next*s. Hardy wants you not just to contemplate but to do.

The book is organized as a series of workshops focused on elements like character or point of view. Each workshop is broken down into a series of sessions, which are in turn broken down into a series of steps. In most cases, these are in the form of questions to ask about the manuscript. One of my favorites in the book helps writers identify a character's flaws and fears, which are important aspects of motivation and conflict:

- What are their flaws?
- What do they fear?
- What are their prejudices?
- What makes them uncomfortable?
- What makes them furious beyond rational thought?
- What makes them change the subject or walk away from a conversation?

I think those last two are particularly revealing. As Hardy points out, they help you identify what your character feels strongly about and what your character might be trying to avoid or repress.

Hardy provides excellent suggestions for how to unclog a "boggy middle," as well as astute questions for diagnosing common problems with endings. She also gives advice on how to evaluate, organize, and prioritize comments from beta readers, critique partners, and editors, which is something I haven't seen in other writing guides.

I think Hardy is less good at explaining the why, and there aren't many examples to help illuminate the dark spots. For authors without much craft knowledge, I'd recommend pairing this book with a more comprehensive guide to novel writing, such as Jessica Brody's *Save the Cat! Writes a Novel* (week fourteen) or Janet Burroway's *Writing Fiction* (week twenty).

When read front to back, Hardy's book feels somewhat repetitive and recursive. The book is an omnibus of what originally appeared as three separate titles, and that explains some of the repetition. While Hardy advises authors to skip around to the areas they need to address and provides some helpful internal links to specific sections, the book does not have a comprehensive table of contents that would allow readers to get straight to the section they need.

However, I think *Revising Your Novel* is also recursive because that is the nature of the revision process itself. Novels are like big shaggy balls of yarn with lots of loose ends, and it's not always clear what will happen if you start pulling on one of those loose threads. Will the novel cohere into a stable and pleasing shape, or will it disintegrate into an untidy pile? It would make life easier if a novel were more like a LEGO construction, which you could consider from all sides before carefully detaching a section and moving it somewhere else. You can strategize, but generally you just have to plunge back into your big ball of words and see what happens. Whichever stage you are in with your novel—drafting, revising, or still dreaming and planning—make some progress this week, however much you can.

WEEK 23
A PAUSE

It is week twenty-three. Remember how last week I advised you to try to keep going with your writing during difficult periods, even if you managed to produce only a little bit? Well, it's also true that there are limits, and sometimes you have to admit it's time to pause. Last week, it was leaf blowers telling me to work through the noise; this week, pneumonia arrived and ordered me to knock it off.

So, rather than a review, this week's essay is a brief reminder that there will be—there should be—weeks when you get nothing accomplished. Sometimes these are planned breaks. Sometimes they are unplanned crises or a sudden blankness in your creative brain.

Banish the guilt and the fear—neither one will serve you—and lean into the rest and the stillness. I've been mulling over a question the writer Jocelyn K. Glei asked on her podcast, *Hurry Slowly*, ever since I heard it: "Who are you without the doing?"[1] Maybe this is a good time for you to circle around this question too. Who are you without the writing? Having some answers will enrich your writing when you come back to it.

WEEK 24

BRIAN SHAWVER, THE LANGUAGE OF FICTION

It is week twenty-four. How did the writing go for you this week? I spent the week recovering from my bout with pneumonia, which meant that only essential work got done. This essay made the cut, but I had to throw out several pounds of cherries that I had planned to use to make jam. I thought a lot about the lost cherries this week and realized that they are a good metaphor for something that happens at a late stage in the writing process, so bear with me for a moment while I tell you more.

My partner and kids and I went and picked these cherries ourselves the day before I came down with pneumonia. It was a foggy day in San Francisco, like most summer days, and we got in the car and drove an hour or so, out from under the blanket of fog, and emerged deep in the East Bay, where it was sunny and warm. We had a picnic and spent a happy hour picking and eating cherries. That night, my partner and I got to work on the stemming and pitting. In a couple hours, we managed to get through about half of our haul.

I love this kind of work, and I love the jamming too. You

need some space in the kitchen and some uninterrupted time, but the work itself is straightforward and enjoyable once you have confidence in what you are doing. Boil the fruit with some sugar until it thickens, ladle it into clean jars, top with lids and bands, and give them a hot water bath to seal them. The kitchen smells heavenly, there is fruit foam skimmed off the top to eat, and at the end you have a row of gorgeous shining jars of homemade jam cooling on your counter. I can even manage it on a weeknight if I order pizza and keep everyone out of the kitchen.

I thought I'd finish up the pitting on Monday and then be ready to jam later in the week. But Monday night, I went from feeling mildly off to feeling feverish and exhausted. I put myself to bed and didn't get out again except for essential tasks for the next three days. The pitted cherries moved to the freezer, and the unpitted cherries got dumped in our giant pasta pot and moved into the fridge.

My partner came down with pneumonia, then one of my kids. That giant pot of cherries sat in the fridge, in the space I needed for juice and Gatorade and chicken soup. I didn't have the energy to pit them; I didn't even have the energy to try to give them away. (Would anyone have wanted our plague cherries?) Day after day, they sat there, quietly decaying and taking up room in my fridge and my brain.

Finally this week, I had enough energy to cook dinner again, and I had to confront the cherries sitting in my pasta pot. I got the pot out of the fridge and picked out a few moldy cherries and a few more overripe ones from the top layer. Probably a third of the pot was salvageable if I could pit them and get them into the freezer right then. I had just enough time and energy to do that or to make the homemade dinner I had planned and which we were all craving after two weeks of takeout. I couldn't do both.

I stood there and looked at the pot for a minute. Then I

poured all of those damn cherries into a paper grocery bag and carried it down to the compost bin in the garage, washed out my pasta pot, filled it with water, and set it on the stove to boil.

Writers, you are going to confront a similar choice at some point during the writing or revision process. You'll realize that the prologue you spent so much time laboring over or the character arc that was part of your original dream for your book just isn't working (sometimes I will be the one to deliver this news), and you'll have to send it to the metaphorical compost bin. It's hard to lose the time and creative energy that you've already invested in these words, but that's just how it goes sometimes. Dump the words, wash out your pot, and then move forward with the work that needs to be done right then to finish your book. Don't get stuck at the decision point or waste your energy on regrets.

Now, on to this week's book, *The Language of Fiction: A Writer's Stylebook* by Brian Shawver. If I've exhausted your patience with the cherry saga, here's the short review: it's fantastic, and I think any fiction writer interested in learning more about how sentences work and how they can improve their own should take the time to read it.

As Shawver points out, *The Language of Fiction* is not a comprehensive grammar or style book, and I think that turns out to be one of its key strengths. Shawver focuses on the issues that matter most to fiction writers. As he puts it: "Language is the water that all writers swim in, and you need to know your element as thoroughly as you can. But it's a big ocean, and mastery for a creative writer involves the knowledge of specific currents and swells."

These currents and swells include the pros and cons of writing in present tense versus past tense, how to format and punctuate dialogue and portray inner thought, when and how to use dialect in dialogue, how to use the past perfect tense to signal time, how to avoid common problems with dangling participial phrases and verb tense shifting, and when and how to violate grammatical rules about sentence fragments and comma splices.

Shawver includes in-depth grammar explanations only when they are necessary to truly understand the subject at hand, and his explanations are clear and well supported by examples, both good and bad. Shawver doesn't have a lot of patience for Strunkian pronouncements such as "Anglo-Saxon is a livelier tongue than Latin, so use Anglo-Saxon words."[1] Instead, he investigates the logic of such statements and then leaves it to you, the writer, to make the choice best suited to your own work.

Perhaps my favorite chapter, if I had to choose just one, is that on adverbs. I agree with Shawver that this useful part of speech has gotten a bum rap in recent years. Shawver argues persuasively that the strongest argument against adverbs isn't that "they're inherently redundant" or "that we can always avoid them by finding more precise verbs or adjectives" but that "they run the risk of disrupting a sentence's eloquence, because of the way most of them are constructed." With care, however, a writer can use the occasional -ly construction with grace and style. As Shawver asks, "You could substitute 'an extremely weak hamster' with 'an etiolated hamster,' or 'he walked slowly' with 'he perambulated,' but is that always a good idea?"

Shawver argues that language is "the most manageably mastered of fiction's mysteries" and suggests that mastery of language can lead to other gains: "Perhaps a control of diction, punctuation, and syntax gives you so many more options for how to say things that you gain access to otherwise inaccessible perceptions." I think that's true, and I think that *The Language of Fiction* can set you on the path toward mastery.

WEEK 25

URSULA K. LE GUIN, STEERING THE CRAFT

It is week twenty-five. Did you do anything to mark the solstice this week? Depending on whether you live in the northern or southern hemisphere, Friday was the longest or shortest day of the year. I love time markers of all kinds, which is why the progression of this little book follows the weeks of the year. It is a reminder that each week is a new opportunity to get something done, to reach a milestone, to start something new, or to just rest in the sun. Every week is a blank page for you to fill.

As Ursula K. Le Guin tells us in this week's book, *Steering the Craft: A Twenty-First-Century Guide to Sailing the Sea of Story*, we have to be ready when the stories find us:

> Some people see art as a matter of control. I see it mostly as a matter of self-control. It's like this: in me there's a story that wants to be told. It is my end; I am its means. If I can keep myself, my ego, my wishes and opinions, my mental junk, out of the way and find the focus of the story, and follow the movement of the story, the story will tell itself.

> Everything I've talked about in this book has to do with being ready to let a story tell itself: having the skills, knowing the craft, so that when the magic boat comes by, you can step into it and guide it where it wants to go, where it ought to go.

Le Guin warns that her book is "not for beginners," and I would agree with that assessment. Le Guin covers many of the expected topics—how to adjust sound and syntax, how to marshal adjectives and adverbs, how to control verb tense and point of view—but she assumes some prior knowledge of all of these topics. Le Guin doesn't just hand us her wisdom on a platter; she often makes us work for it. In some sections, a well-chosen example or two are all the explanation we get. In others, we are asked to learn by doing exercises, which Le Guin follows with advice in the guise of critique notes or questions.

Le Guin does provide clear and helpful guidance on the crucial question of whether to choose past or present tense for your story: "I see the big difference between the past and present tenses not as immediacy but as complexity and size of field. A story told in the present tense is necessarily focused on action in a single time and therefore a single place. Use of the past tense(s) allows continual referring back and forth in time and space. . . . The difference is like the difference between a narrow-beam flashlight and sunlight. One shows a small, intense, brightly lit field with nothing around it; the other shows the world." As she notes, present tense is currently in vogue, especially in young adult fiction, but you should base your choice on the needs of your story.

The book's best chapter is that on point of view. Le Guin is clear and systematic in this chapter. She defines seven different points of view—first person, limited third person, involved (omniscient) author, detached author, and observer-narrator in first person and third person—and describes the advantages and limitations of each. Even better, she creates a tiny scene and rewrites it in each of the points of view, which gives you an immediate feel for how each one works. I think this chapter alone is worth the price of the book.

Le Guin describes *Steering the Craft* as a workbook, and the exercises, which she calls "consciousness-raisers," are the best I've seen. As she says, "There's luck in art. And there's the gift. You can't earn that. But you can learn skill, you can earn it. You can learn to deserve your gift." If you want to develop a writing course for yourself or for a group, I think starting with the exercises in Janet Burroway's *Writing Fiction*, if you are more interested in structure, or Brian Shawver's *The Language of Fiction*, if you are more interested in sentences, and then moving to Le Guin's book would be an excellent way to proceed. Le Guin also provides an entire chapter with useful guidance on how to run a successful peer critique group.

Le Guin is enjoyably tart on some topics ("*Somehow* is a super-weasel, a word that betrays that the author didn't want to bother thinking out the story"; "the adjective or qualifier *fucking* is a really big tick"; "Too many people who yatter on about 'you should never use the passive voice' don't even know what it is"), but she also believes that nothing is off limits to authors. As she notes, "Good and careful writers will blow all Rules of Writing into bits." She is also, as I expected, scrupulously neutral when it comes to the literary fiction–genre fiction divide we have traced in other writers, nor does she take sides in the great plotter versus pantser debate: "If you aren't a planner or a plotter, don't worry. The world's full of stories . . . . I like my image of 'steering the craft,' but in fact the story boat is a magic one. It knows its course. The job of the person at the helm is to help it find its own way to wherever it's going." Doesn't that sound relaxing? You might be in charge, but the boat will save you from drowning if you don't have a direction yet and just need to drift until you do.

WEEK 26
CRAFT BOOK TAXONOMY

It is week twenty-six. My question for you this week: How has the writing gone this year? Take a minute to recognize what you've achieved during the last six months, even if it is less than you had hoped or planned—especially if it is less than you had hoped or planned. There are twenty-six weeks left in the year. What could you accomplish if you started something today and then spent time on it every week?

I'm taking time this week to recognize what I've accomplished in my own writing over the last six months. Before starting this project, I read craft books and wrote blog posts when I had an unexpected chunk of free time, which wasn't often. Every year, I told myself I would do more, and every year I did about the same—read a few books, wrote a handful of posts.

This year, I did three things differently: first, I publicly committed to showing my work; second, I created time in my schedule for the reading and writing I needed to do; and third, I made my progress visible for myself by hanging it on the wall near my desk. If you've gotten stuck or have stalled out before even starting, consider trying these methods and see if they work for you. (These methods were inspired by artist and writer Austin Kleon, business coach Ashley Gartland, and author and podcaster Jocelyn K. Glei—check out their work and see if they inspire you too.)

I want to take a moment now to survey what I've read over the last six months. I've begun mentally organizing writing craft books into three broad categories:

- **Inspirers**. These are books that teach us about creativity or about the habits and mind-set of writers. They can also be books that ask what a novel is, like Jane Smiley's *13 Ways of Looking at the Novel*. This is the category you turn to when your well is dry and you need inspiration or commiseration from creators who have been in that stuck place and can help you get out.
- **Systematizers**. These are books that analyze story structure or writing methods and provide concrete and specific guidance on how to shape a story or finish a novel. If you need guidance on how to untangle a plot, craft a better character arc, or plot or pants your way to the finish line, these are the books you turn to.
- **Crafters**. These are books that give instruction on the nitty-gritty details of how to revise, how to control point of view and voice, and how to polish sentences. You can use these books to practice your craft or to guide you in adding the finishing touches to a rough draft.

Somewhere around week seventeen, I realized I had been unconsciously (and naively) searching for The One Writing Craft Book to Rule Them All and had to recognize that I wouldn't find it, although some books fall into multiple categories. The truth is you are going to need different things at different stages in a project. At the end of the book, you'll find a list of my recommendations that will help you find the book that will meet you where you are and take you where you want to go.

WEEK 27
HOW TO READ A BOOK

It is week twenty-seven. I'll pick up the book reviews again next week, but right now I want to give you some tips about how to read a nonfiction book efficiently. Of course, efficiency is not always your goal. Sometimes you need to do a thorough, deep, concentrated read of a complex book that you already know will have a lot of impact on your work or life. And sometimes you just want to take your time and enjoy the material.

But when you are researching or learning about a topic, most books will fall into a middle category. You know enough from the title or blurb or a recommendation to believe that the book will be useful, but you won't know for sure until you dive in. What I'm going to show you now is how to quickly absorb what a book has to teach you and how to take notes so that you can add the book to your personal knowledge database.

I like to start by setting my intentions for my reading. Reread the blurb, on the back cover or online, and think about what you hope to learn from this book. You can even write down your intention at the top of your notes, which will help you stay focused. (For example, *I want to learn more about point of view because so far I've only used third-person limited in my writing, and I'd like to experiment with other options.*) If the book has been sitting in your to-be-read pile for years, make sure you still think you will benefit from it. If you've moved on, take the book to the nearest Little Free Library and go on to the next. You are not in school and no one has assigned you this book. The first rule of efficient reading is to stop immediately if the book isn't fulfilling the intentions you set.

Next, you want to get the lay of the land, just like you would do when visiting a city for the first time. Read through the table of contents carefully and make a mental or physical note about which sections interest you most. (If you are reading on an e-reader, you'll automatically be taken to the beginning of the text, but make the effort to get back to the table of contents.) Are there exercises or checklists you want to use, now or in the future? Is there material you think you can skip or skim?

For example, looking at the table of contents for Jessica Brody's *Save the Cat! Writes a Novel* tells me that chapter 1 expands on the overview in the introduction; chapter 2 is where Brody lays out the beat sheet, which I know from the blurb is the heart of the book; chapter 3 is an overview of genre; chapters 4 through 13 are about specific genres or kinds of stories; and chapters 14 and 15 are about how to write pitches and handle other very specific writing and publishing tasks. Just from studying these couple of pages, I now have a mental outline of the whole book, and I also have a reading plan: I'm going to skim the introduction and chapter 1, I'm going to read chapters 2 and 3 closely, and then I'm going to read chapters 4 through the end strategically, choosing those that I think will teach me what I want to learn. If I wrote romance, for example, I might skip or skim the chapter on horror.

Now you are ready to start reading. If this is a chapter you've planned to skim, use section headers and the first sentences of paragraphs like rocks you are landing on as you skip across a river. If you feel sure of your footing, hop forward. If you need to catch your balance or just look around, read every word. When you come to an example, skip it for now if you already understand the principle it illustrates. Remember to keep checking in with your intentions and alter your reading plan if you find something unexpectedly valuable (or worthless). Not every word of every book is going to be helpful for you.

As you go, highlight sentences where the author summarizes or recaps a section or chapter. When you come across a section that is especially helpful, highlight the section header or make a note in the table of contents. Track your thoughts as you read and include them in your notes. Does this author disagree with another author you've read? Does the material raise a question you want to investigate further? Do you just need to say, "WTF?"

When you reach the end of the book, list in your notes the things that you found valuable or may want to come back to. For example, my bottom-of-the-notes list for Chuck Wendig's *Damn Fine Story* looks like this:

- Fantastic list of plot moves to fix a "mushy middle"
- Clear explanation of relationship between character and plot
- Book is funny, inclusive; has top-shelf cursing

If you have written physical notes, collect all of them in one place where you can refer back to them easily. If you are highlighting and taking notes on an e-reader, figure out how to copy and paste them into another program. (Remember, always, that what Amazon giveth, Amazon can taketh away. That handy Kindle highlights page may not be around forever.) This is your knowledge database that you will return to when you are starting a new book and trying to decide whether to use first- or third-person point of view (who had the best discussion of that?) or when you are revising and want to remember what you learned about strong verbs (what was that great thing Connie Hale said about them?).

I learned these strategies during my many (many, many) years of grad school. In addition to reading mammoth Victorian novels in the space of a week, I also needed to read and absorb an enormous amount of secondary material. If I had read every single word of every book and article I needed to know about, I would still be working on my dissertation or, more likely, would have given up long ago. Now these strategies are yours.

WEEK 28
K. M. WEILAND, OUTLINING YOUR NOVEL

It is week twenty-eight. I'm settled back in at my desk after a two-week road trip from Vermont to North Carolina. The trip was glorious but almost too full of sights, sounds, sensations, and tastes. I wouldn't have missed any of it—the maple creemees or the Pat's cheesesteak or the Carolina barbecue; kayaking on Lake Champlain at sunset; listening to Jeff Tweedy sing "Noah's Flood" in a sudden summer shower; or traveling with five of my favorite humans in a giant white whale of an SUV—but it feels good to be back in my beloved San Francisco, which has been muffled in a deep, cool layer of soothing fog all week.

Now let's get into this week's book, *Outlining Your Novel: Map Your Way to Success* by K. M. Weiland. Reading Weiland's book this week, I found myself itching to return to my own novel, and I think that's one benefit of books like these that are very focused on process. The combination of clear steps and the imperative mood (first, do this; next, do that) is both motivational and approachable.

Weiland's method is as good as any I've seen so far. She guides you through a series of steps to identify your premise, central conflict, key scenes, character backstories, and setting details before pulling it all together into an outline that will guide your first draft. The big strength of Weiland's approach is that, at each stage, she emphasizes exploration. Using techniques like brainstorming and freewriting, she sorts through any number of possible ideas in order to find the best direction for her story. For example, at the very beginning, she throws "what if" questions at her premise: "Once you've selected the few ideas that might work, start looking for tangents: 'If such and such happened, then what if this also happened? Or what if this happened instead?'"

Whenever you are stuck, Weiland advises, try restating the problem as a question. "The princess is trapped in the high tower" becomes "How can I get the princess out of the high tower?" Throughout the book, Weiland offers lists of questions for each stage of the outlining process. Her questions about character and her chapter about character interviews are particularly valuable. I also think her idea about "reverse outlining" is useful, especially when you are trying to work out what needs to happen in the middle of your book. As Weiland says, "When you can work your way backwards from a known point, finding your way becomes as simple as filling in the blanks." Going back to the princess example—you know *a* next step, that she is freed from the tower, you just don't know the one right before it.

Weiland notes at the beginning of the book that no one method, hers included, will work for every writer: "Even if a particular method or routine works for one author, that singular success doesn't make it a universal principle." The book includes interviews with other authors about their own methods, allowing readers to glean alternate approaches. Weiland also includes big chunks from her own outlines, which are great fun to read. An outline, in Weiland's method, is not a sterile, rigid structure but rather a freewheeling idea laboratory for your book.

Once you've got an outline in hand, Weiland reminds us, there is no rule that you have to stick to it if you make new discoveries during the drafting process. Having that outline, however, can provide the psychological reassurance you need to stave off writer's block and keep moving forward. I heard an interview this week with the wonderful Meg Wolitzer on *The Secret Library* podcast (which I highly recommend) during which she likened outlines to EpiPens: "You might not need it, but it's nice to know you have it."[1] Even if you are a confirmed pantser, consider giving Weiland's method a try for your next project.

WEEK 29

JAMES SCOTT BELL, WRITE YOUR NOVEL FROM THE MIDDLE

It is week twenty-nine. I was deep in the midst of two different copyediting projects this week, happily polishing sentences, looking up words in *Merriam-Webster*, confirming facts on Google, and checking rules in the *Chicago Manual of Style* (ranch hand, not ranch-hand; Michael Jackson's ranch is indeed called Neverland; a last name with a *de* prefix is capitalized only when it begins a sentence) until I inadvertently broke all of my macros in Microsoft Word.

Macros are handy little pieces of code that allow me to highlight a word or phrase in my document and, with one keystroke, query it in *Merriam-Webster* or Google or send it to the term list of the book's style sheet. I spent a few minutes trying to limp along without them, then another few minutes cursing, before I took a deep breath and went through the process to reinstall them and tweak them for my preferences. It was a good reminder of how much I value these little tools and how glad I am that I learned the basics of how to work with them well enough that I could restore them without too much angst. Lesson: take a moment to appreciate the tools you depend on for your writing. Make sure you have backups and know how to use them so that whenever you encounter the inevitable technological hiccup, you won't get stuck.

Now, on to this week's book, *Write Your Novel from the Middle: A New Approach for Plotters, Pantsers and Everyone in Between* by James Scott Bell. This pithy little book will cost you four dollars and an hour of your time, and I think it's well worth the investment. Bell, a thriller author and writing instructor, offers up a new way of thinking about the familiar three-act structure.

He has two key insights: First, plot structure is like a suspension bridge, anchored by the initial problem the main character must confront at one end of the bridge and by the climactic battle (literal or metaphorical) at the other end. Second, there is a "Mirror Moment" at the midpoint of the plot:

> At this point in the story, the character looks at himself. He takes stock of where he is in the conflict and—depending on the type of story—has either of two basic thoughts. In a character-driven story, he looks at himself and wonders what kind of person he is. What is he becoming? If he continues the fight of Act II, how will he be different? What will he have to do to overcome his inner challenges? How will he have to change in order to battle successfully? The second type of look is more for plot-driven fiction. It's where the character looks at himself and considers the odds against him. At this point the forces seem so vast that there is virtually no way to go on and not face certain death. That death can be physical, professional, or psychological.

Bell goes on to argue that if you start by crafting the Mirror Moment, it will help you work out both what comes before it and what must come after it. How did this character get into this position? And how will they get out? What is the backstory that made this character who they are? And what is the transformation this character will have to undergo to resolve the story?

As Bell points out, zeroing in on this moment can work for all writers: "You can explore this moment at any time in your writing process. You can play with it, tweak it. Whether you are a plotter or pantser, just thinking about what the 'look in the mirror' might reveal will help you bring depth and cohesion to your novel." He also provides specific guidance on how this method could work for different kinds of writers, at different stages in the planning or drafting process.

One of my favorite aspects of the book is that we get to see an experienced novelist and teacher going right to the source—stories—and coming back to tell us what he has found. He was curious about what a midpoint was and how it fit into the three-act structure, and so he opened up his favorite novels and cued up his favorite films at the middle and then analyzed what he found. At the end of the book, he also takes us on a tour of a brilliantly executed but little-known 1950s noir novel to show us how it works.

These methods are available to you too! Spend a weekend poking around on your shelves and analyzing your favorite novels. They aren't made from magic; they are made from words. With time, attention, and effort, you can learn how the masters use these tools and bring those lessons to your own work.

WEEK 30
JANE ALISON, MEANDER, SPIRAL, EXPLODE

It is week thirty. How did the writing go this week? It's midsummer, a time of year that isn't always good for brain work. You may be smothering under a blanket of heat (come enjoy the San Francisco fog!) or distracted by a vacation or a different schedule. If you need a refreshing tonic to wake your creative brain, then this week's book might be the one for you.

In *Meander, Spiral, Explode: Design and Pattern in Narrative*, Jane Alison sets out to explore patterns other than the classic wave or arc structure. Why, she asks, has the dramatic arc, which has its origins in Greek tragedy, become the dominant form of the novel, our most flexible and "cannibalistic" genre? Her hope, summarized in the final words of the book, is that "other patterns might help us imagine new ways to make our narratives vital and true, keep making our novels novel."

Before exploring these patterns, Alison gives us a tour through what she sees as the elements of fiction: point, line, texture; movement and flow; and color. These early chapters will alert you to alternate ways of experiencing a text. Here, for example, is Alison on texture and white space: "Glancing at a page, we first see text as texture: marks in a white field leave enough space to feel airy or form dense blocks, even weighted with a sludge of footnotes." Writers often add paragraph breaks during action scenes to increase the feeling of pace. What Alison points out is that the additional white space supports that feeling of streamlined speed.

Alison's choice of patterns follows those identified by Peter Stevens, in his book *Patterns in Nature*, as "nature's darlings":

> SPIRAL: think of a fiddlehead fern, whirlpool, hurricane, horns twisting from a ram's head, or a chambered nautilus. MEANDER: picture a river curving and kinking, a snake in motion, a snail's silver trail, or the path left by a goat grazing the tenderest greens. RADIAL or EXPLOSION: a splash of dripping water, petals growing from a daisy's heart, light radiating from the sun, the ring left around a tick bite. BRANCHING and other FRACTAL patterns: self-replication at lesser scale, made by trees, coastlines, clouds. And CELLULAR patterns: repeating shapes you see in a honeycomb, foam of bubbles, cracked lakebed, or light rippling in a pool; these can look like cells or, inversely, like a net.

Alison describes her book as "a museum of specimens," and that feels exactly right. We move through "rooms" of texts, grouped by pattern, with Alison as our delighted and appreciative guide. Alison herself is an inventive prose stylist, and I found this book a pure joy to read.

I also had the pleasure this week of participating in a discussion about the book with a group of smart, insightful women and was reminded of how much a good discussion can wake up your brain and make the sparks fly. If you have a writers' group (or want to convene an ad hoc group), *Meander, Spiral, Explode* will generate a vigorous discussion.

Our group spent a lot of time considering how to entice readers to engage with experimental forms. One participant pointed out that curiosity—keeping the reader wondering—is key, and this answer was echoed by Alison herself, who sent in taped responses to the group's questions. Writers, Alison pointed out, "are going to engage the kind of reader they want"—readers who want to know *Who is this person?* and *What is the language doing?*, not just *What happens next?* All writers want readers who "have respect for another person's brain," readers who will follow you as you figure something out in your work.

Even if you plan to stick to the classic arc form in your own novel, reading *Meander, Spiral, Explode* can help enliven your writing by showing you opportunities to construct meaning that you hadn't seen before. It will give you ideas about how to speed up and slow down, about how to use color as a pattern, about how to use words to pull your reader through your book.

I think Alison's patterns could also be used as a creative playground of sorts. What would happen if you recast your story as a spiral or an explosion? What would be at the center of that spiral? What would be the energy driving the explosion or the match that ignited it? If you took one of your characters and sent them off on a meandering path, where would they go? Doing these experiments, in thought or in writing, can help you get to know your characters and your plot better and get the creative juices flowing again when you are feeling stagnant.

WEEK 31

DEAN WESLEY SMITH, WRITING INTO THE DARK

It is week thirty-one. I'm camping in the redwoods this weekend and bringing along a fresh new legal pad and my favorite pens in the hopes that I can do some scribbling and planning for my novel, which is just starting to come into focus. I always bring along a notebook when I camp, even if I don't have a project in mind. Something about being untethered from my screens and my daily habits unlocks the creative bits of my brain that otherwise prefer to stay silent.

This week's book, *Writing into the Dark: How to Write a Novel without an Outline* by Dean Wesley Smith, is so radically different in style and temperament from Jane Alison's *Meander, Spiral, Explode*, which I reviewed last week, that the juxtaposition made my head spin. The book, apparently a collection of mashed-together blog posts, is full of repetition and digressions. It is perhaps not the best exemplar of what you can hope to accomplish while writing into the dark, but I very much doubt Smith gives a fuck, and that is one of the charms of the book. He's just a writer (a very practiced one) telling you what works for him. He seems to care more about attacking the English teachers he sets up as straw men than he does about whether anyone adopts his methods.

Let's see what these methods boil down to:

- Get started by putting a character into a scene and climbing into their head. "Don't allow yourself to type one word that doesn't come from the character's opinion or sensory feelings or emotions."
- Write the next sentence. Just keep going. "Suck it up and write the next sentence. And then the next." But that next sentence doesn't necessarily have to be the next sentence as the reader will encounter it.
- You can jump forward in time. If you know what's going to happen in a later scene but don't know how you are going to get there, jump to that scene and start writing. You can go back and fill in the gap later. Smith calls this learning how to be "unstuck in time" in your novel.
- You can go back to what you've already written. If you can't see the next sentence yet, go back to an earlier point of the book and move forward, adding and revising, until you've built up momentum to vault you past the white space. Smith calls this "cycling."
- Outline as you go. After you finish a scene, write a quick note about what happened in the scene and where you left your characters. You can use this outline to quickly pick up from where you left off (particularly useful for novels with multiple points of view) or diagnose where you might have taken a wrong turn in your plot.

- Be willing to write into dead ends and then cut the material. Sometimes you have to explore the terrain to find the best path. And all writing is practice and therefore valuable. "When you are writing new words, you are never wasting your time."
- Revise as you go. Smith proclaims, "YOU ARE NOT GOING TO REWRITE THE BOOK," (yes, in all caps) and thus doesn't want you to write a sloppy draft the first time through. What he actually does, however, is revise as he goes, through his cycling method.
- If you get stuck, you may have written past the ending of a scene. Go back and read the scene and see if you spot a natural ending point. If so, cut off the extra material and start a new scene.

I cannot tell you if these tactics will work for you (and my editor's brain and Virgo soul are both fretting over Smith's stance on revision), but I do think that many of his methods are worth a try for you pantsers out there—perhaps for the plotters too. And Smith himself would be the first to tell you to adapt them to your own purposes (which this editor will tell you should include revision).

WEEK 32
JUNE CASAGRANDE, IT WAS THE BEST OF SENTENCES, IT WAS THE WORST OF SENTENCES

It is week thirty-two. Just as I had hoped, I sat down among the redwoods last weekend to spin out ideas for my novel. I tried to use K. M. Weiland's outlining formula but realized that I don't yet know enough about my characters and setting to productively answer those *why* questions, so I'm going to do some more thinking and gathering before trying again. These waning days of summer are perfect for the kind of aimless reading and daydreaming that lead to flashes of inspiration way down the road when you've forgotten to expect them.

This week's book—June Casagrande's *It Was the Best of Sentences, It Was the Worst of Sentences: A Writer's Guide to Crafting Killer Sentences*—is the opposite of aimless and daydreamy. This is a book of short sentences, sharp angles, and clear advice. Casagrande's aim is to make you a better writer, not to teach you grammar—the grammar instruction is just something that happens along the way. Like learning about dovetail joints in the course of making a table, you will learn about relative clauses in the course of creating strong sentences. You will always know the *why* before she explains the *how*.

For example, she kicks off the book by demonstrating how to use subordination to highlight the main point of your sentence. Consider this example: "Before robbing a bank, Mike was an accountant." Tacking on the subordinating conjunction *before* diminishes the power of the bank robbery, giving Mike's status as an accountant the grammatical starring role in the sentence. Consider this change: "After twenty-five years as an accountant, Mike robbed a bank." Once you understand this principle, you can use the subordination lever to bring down the house lights and spotlight your main point. There's no better or worse in this example—it depends on what you want to emphasize.

Casagrande treats relative clauses, prepositional phrases, and participial phrases in a similar way, showing you how to use them to add detail to sentences while avoiding the dreaded danglers and misplaced modifiers. Here's a dangler for you: "Walking down the beach, Theo's shoulders got sunburned." Theo's shoulders weren't walking down the beach—it was Theo or his feet. To fix: "Walking down the beach, Theo got a sunburn on his shoulders."

Casagrande is a journalist and, though she also covers fiction, she is more focused on clarity than art. She prefers short sentences and has no use for semicolons. (Her choice of a cumbersome title referencing the famously long and complex opening sentence of Dickens's *Tale of Two Cities* feels a bit off-brand.) Yet she is far from being a dictator: "Every one of the writing 'rules' you hear is rooted in a good idea with at least some practical application. Yet none of these rules is worth a damn when stretched into an absolute." Instead, she advises, "think of them not as rules but as safe havens. If you're getting into trouble with a long sentence, you can chop it into shorter sentences. If your adverb-laden sentence falls flat, you can just ditch the adverbs."

In other words, get down to the basics: What is the main action in this sentence? That's your verb. Who is doing the action? That's your subject. What is this thing you are talking about? That's your noun, to be placed wherever it will fit best. Clarify these elements for yourself, and the sentence will straighten out.

Although Casagrande gives you permission to ignore the rules, she insists that you cannot ignore the reader. "Your writing is not about you. It's about the Reader. Even when it's quite literally about you—in memoirs, personal essays, first-person accounts—it's not really about you." This doesn't mean that you have to force your story into a path you think your ideal reader will approve or tamp down your distinctive voice. But it does mean that you need to try to read your writing like a reader would, especially during revision. Casagrande's book will help you do just that.

WEEK 33

FRANCINE PROSE, READING LIKE A WRITER

It is week thirty-three. How did the writing go this week? Are you beset by distractions, like back-to-school to-do lists and new schedules? Or recovering from or embarking on a summer vacation? The clarity and renewed vigor I always associate with September is right around the corner, so muddle through these last hazy weeks of summer as best you can. Or don't muddle through them at all; rather, drift happily and lazily through the days.

Whatever these upcoming weeks hold for you, Francine Prose's *Reading Like a Writer: A Guide for People Who Love Books and for Those Who Want to Write Them* would make a good companion. It's a book that will reward either sustained attention or aimless browsing. You can jump in wherever you like—perhaps starting with the particularly illuminating chapters on gesture or details—and then spin away into whatever excursion Prose inspires: maybe a quick dip into a Flannery O'Connor story or a sustained soak in Henry James's *Portrait of a Lady*.

Prose's book does exactly what the title promises. She shows you how to read closely and critically by modeling what that looks like. She quotes long passages and then takes them apart, examining the effects of the writer's choices. As Prose describes her method: "Ask yourself what sort of information each word—each word choice—is conveying." Her examination of this passage from Jane Austen's *Sense and Sensibility* is a good example of her method:

> He was not an ill-disposed young man, unless to be rather cold hearted, and rather selfish, is to be ill-disposed: but he was, in general, well respected; for he conducted himself with propriety in the discharge of his ordinary duties. Had he married a more amiable woman, he might have been made still more respectable than he was: he might even have been made amiable himself; for he was very young when he married, and very fond of his wife. But Mrs. John Dashwood was a strong caricature of himself;—more narrow-minded and selfish.

And Prose's analysis:

> Part of what's so delightful about the paragraph is how the narrator seems to be making such an effort to be fair and to present such a balanced view of the John Dashwoods that she begins by denying that he is "ill-disposed" but only "rather selfish and rather cold hearted"—adjectives far more damning than "ill-disposed." . . . Again, in the apparent interest of fairness, the narrator explains how Mr. Dashwood might have been more amiable "had he married a more amiable woman." And even as we are distracted by considering the truth of the observation about how readily the faults of one spouse can rub off on the other, particularly if they marry when they are young and in love, and how it sometimes happens that one partner can come to seem like a caricature of the other, Austen zeroes in for the kill and

effectively finishes off the conniving Mrs. Dashwood. Gone is all pretense of fairness: Mrs. John Dashwood is simply more narrow-minded and more selfish.

This passage appears in Prose's chapter about character, and it is typical of her method. She eschews categories or systems or principles, preferring to start instead from examples. As she says about character, "Whatever we may think we know about the best way to create a character, literature shows us that it differs from writer to writer, sometimes from book to book." There are no generalities or models; instead, there are possible trails to follow—but only if you choose. Prose delights in showing us that all writing rules "can be circumvented by any writer skillful enough to get away with it." (Just as, you may remember, Casagrande argued in *It Was the Best of Sentences*, which I reviewed last week.)

Prose's goal is for you, the writer, to build your own "private lessons in the art of fiction" by reading—and, crucially, rereading—the works that inspire, delight, confound, and humble you. Prose is oriented to literary fiction and to the traditional European and American canon. Your own inspirations may lie elsewhere. Whatever it is you read, Prose's point is that you should read it closely and repeatedly. This is something that anyone who teaches fiction knows: you may believe that your tenth reading of a work will yield nothing new, and then you sit down to read and find you were wrong. So if you are at loose ends over the next couple of weeks, follow Prose's model: pull a favorite novel down off the shelf, read it closely, and find out what it can teach you about how to write.

WEEK 34
CHRISTOPHER CASTELLANI, THE ART OF PERSPECTIVE

It is week thirty-four. I came across a mindfulness exercise this week—on David Cain's wonderful blog *Raptitude*—that seems custom-built for writers. Cain calls it "dying on purpose," and it involves "looking at the scene in front of you as though it's happening without you."[1] Try to hover above it and to remove your own reactions and judgments and just observe.

From a mindfulness perspective, this exercise is helpful because it can quiet your brain, muting anxiety and other negative reactions. As Cain puts it, "It's just stuff happening, not stuff happening *to you*." For a writer, this exercise can give you practice with perspective, trying on an omniscient-narrator gaze that sees everything and feels nothing. You could also take the exercise one step further after getting this cleansing distance by zooming back in to the perspective of other "characters" in the scene. Looking around the coffee shop in which I'm writing, I wonder: What does the bored-looking barista wish he were doing? What's on the mind of the woman frowning at her phone? What are the friends in the corner laughing about? Where is the man ordering the two iced horchata lattes going when he leaves? Each of these participants in the scene would tell a different story about it, colored by their perspective of what is happening to them.

This is precisely the topic Christopher Castellani delves into in his thought-provoking book, *The Art of Perspective: Who Tells the Story*. As Castellani points out, "There is no more important decision the writer makes than who tells the story, because, whoever that narrator is, he will compel us to tell it his way, with his frames of reference, his agenda and lexicon and baggage, within his particular wedge of time. Every narrator becomes the story, and the story becomes him." Familiar stories retold from the perspective of a character who is on the margin in the original are the most dramatic examples of this principle: the "madwoman in the attic" from Charlotte Brontë's *Jane Eyre* gaining control of the narrative in Jean Rhys's *Wide Sargasso Sea*; the Wicked Witch of the West retelling the story of *The Wizard of Oz* in *Wicked*; J. M. Coetzee dropping another character onto the island with Robinson Crusoe and Friday in *Foe*.

However, most choices about perspective are more nuanced and therefore more difficult to understand and control. Castellani does have some wisdom to offer about the consequences of a big decision like the choice between a first-person and a third-person narrator:

> A character who narrates in first person exposes herself to a greater degree than she would in third person. The relative distance of third person gives her cover; and, of course, as we have seen, even within third person the narrator can modulate that distance. With the intimacy of first person comes a vulnerability for which there is little or no cover, and with that vulnerability comes both a more exciting opportunity to win the reader's engagement and a higher risk of rejection.

Consider the kind of relationship you want to create between your narrator and your reader, and allow that to influence your decision about point of view.

Castellani is more interested in tracking subtle narrative levers, such as distance. His method is very like that of Francine Prose, whose book *Reading Like a Writer* I discussed last week: he takes a close look at how specific books work. "If there are such things as answers or secrets when it comes to how to tell good stories, they have already been told to us by the narrators of the novels and stories that have charged and changed us. Have we been paying attention?" Castellani will show you how to pay attention, what to look for, as you follow him through works by E. M. Forster, Lorrie Moore, William Faulkner, and others. As with Prose's techniques, you can bring these reading strategies to works that resonate with you or that you particularly want to learn from.

Castellani has thoughtful things to say about current literary trends. He notes, for example, that "the 'unreliable narrator' label is being applied not only to the obviously deluded first-person speaker, but also to the third-person narrator who exhibits even a smidgen of a personality. An attitude, if you will. . . . Implicit in this is the recognition, however subconscious, that all stories are constructed, and that the person telling the story always brings to it his biases and sensibility . . . . That what makes every narrator essentially unreliable is the simple fact of his humanity."

This same distrust of the notion of absolute truth has led novelists to reject the traditional nineteenth-century narrator, who was "more comfortable with the burden of omniscience," Castellani argues. "Instead, our charge has been to depict individual experience in its fullest and most vivid detail, keeping in the back of our minds that that experience is itself inherently limited." Castellani notes that the use of multiple third-person narrators is a kind of omniscience, but one in which "the friction among the characters produces much of the meaning, which must be inferred or interpreted by the reader rather than provided by the omniscient narrator." However, just because the narrative authority is broken up into bright, prismatic shards, doesn't mean it's not there: "There may not be a chummy or imperious or oracular or cynical voice that serves as a stand-in for the author, but the text asserts its authority nonetheless" through a multitude of decisions about how long characters get to hold the narrative mic, which scenes they get to tell us, and how close we are to them.

In discussing his own relationship with perspective—both in the context of a novel he is trying to write and of a memory he is trying to understand—Castellani makes the profound point that our struggles with perspective boil down to "its refusal to keep still." We know from reflecting on our own lives that many things—the passage of time, changing goals and dreams, new knowledge—can influence the way we view the events that have shaped us. If meaning can always be changing in this way, how do we ever know what is true? As a writer, "When will I know if I have the 'right' perspective to make the best possible story from that raw material? And, if I do find the 'right' perspective, will it lead me reliably to an effective narrative strategy?" The answer is, as you suspected, that you will never know. The only thing to do is to try. Write your way through and out.

As Castellani puts it: "The writer's goal is not to derive comfort from the trek across the sea and up the mountain, but to document that view with honesty and integrity once she gets there. In other words, to use the tools of craft to tell the story with as much urgency and insight and style and depth as she can. In that telling is, of course, where the art of perspective lies." And perspective—your perspective, your specific gaze—is what will bring new life to old stories.

WEEK 35
DAVID LYNCH, CATCHING THE BIG FISH

It is week thirty-five. This is the sentence where I often ask you how the writing is going. I'm not going to do that this week because this week is different. This is the first week of Fuck It Fall, which I am going to tell you all about after I warn you that there is going to be an extra amount of cursing in this essay. (Also, I happen to be writing this on my birthday, and so I get to do whatever the fuck I want. Isn't that the point of birthdays?)

Here in San Francisco, fall is the time when the cold gray blanket of fog that has covered the city all summer gets whisked off over the ocean as the sun pours down over the hills that are now the color of a lion's coat. The whole world is blue and gold, with the rich shadows and mellow light of early fall. The sunset-red of the Golden Gate Bridge becomes so achingly beautiful against the blue sky and the golden hills that it could stop your heart.

If you are a parent of school-aged children, fall is also the time when you get back into a schedule and when that schedule still feels fresh and welcome and you aren't yet tired to death of fucking lunchboxes and forms and school assemblies. If you are a parent of school-aged children who works at home, fall is the time when you rediscover the golden quality of the silence in your home when you are the only one in it.

If you are a parent, one who is newly single, and you become fast friends with another newly single parent, you might decide that fall is a good time to be a tiny bit selfish and to say no to some of the should-dos and yes to some of the could-dos, for no better reason than because you fucking want to, and that might be how Fuck It Fall is born.

And you might find that, year after year, Fuck It Fall is a state of mind you need to experience because it reminds you that the year is dying and we are all dying (as slowly as we possibly can, but still dying) and that this needs to be the end of thinking and the beginning of doing.

You may be wondering how all of this relates to writing. And, you may wonder, how many more times can this woman possibly say "fuck"? The answers are: one, I'm about to fucking tell you; and two, lots.

If you are filmmaker David Lynch—author of this week's book, *Catching the Big Fish: Meditation, Consciousness, and Creativity*—you can tell your readers that meditation can help them shed the "Suffocating Rubber Clown Suit of Negativity" and deliver them to "an ocean of pure consciousness," where they will find bliss but also ideas: "Little fish swim on the surface, but the big ones swim down below. If you can expand the container you're fishing in—your consciousness—you can catch bigger fish."

Also, if you are David Lynch, you can write a chapter titled "The Box and the Key," the only words of which are, "I don't have a clue what those are." And because you are David Lynch, and this is a book about consciousness and the mysteries of creativity, this pronouncement seems, to one reader at least, not like nonsense but like a koan reminding us to hold space for inspiration even when the fish refuse to take your bait.

And if you are David Lynch, you can spend years making *Eraserhead* and, at a particularly low point, when it feels as if maybe the only way you will be able to finish it is to substitute stop-motion characters for actors, your "very responsible" brother and father sit you down in a "dark living room" and tell you to give up and get a job, and you do get a job delivering the *Wall Street Journal* for fifty bucks a week and use that money to complete the movie a scene at a time. Then, years later, you can find out that Stanley Kubrick, one of your heroes, invited some film crew guys over to his house to watch his favorite film, and it is *Eraserhead*.

And if you are David Lynch, you can be filming in Italy and happen to hear that Federico Fellini, another of your heroes, has been hospitalized, and you know a couple of friends of his who happen to stop by and agree to bring you with them when they visit, and you get to sit down next to Fellini in his hospital room and hear him talk about film, and two days later he slips into a coma he never comes out of.

I spent a lot of time while reading this book wondering if David Lynch could do all of these things because he is David Lynch, or if he is David Lynch because he can do these things. I'm pretty sure it's the latter.

What does this mean for you? It means that you need to gird your loins and hoist your tits and say fuck you to every imposter-syndrome demon and time-sucking monster that dares to confront you because this is Fuck It Fall, and it is time for you to write your book.

Find the room of your own. Find your mantra. Shed that Suffocating Rubber Clown Suit of Negativity. Dive into that ocean of consciousness teeming with idea fish. Figure out what the box and the key are for. Insist on being taken to fucking Fellini on his fucking deathbed. Whatever it takes, start fishing for those ideas. Start taking yourself seriously if you haven't yet done so.

This is the time. There is no other time.

WEEK 36
JACK BICKHAM, ELEMENTS OF FICTION WRITING

It is week thirty-six. How did the writing go this week? Did you come back creaky after a long vacation, or did you jump right into Fuck It Fall? Whichever it was, embrace the fresh new week ahead of you and block out time to do something creative. If you are still fishing for ideas, try out some of Twyla Tharp's exercises from *The Creative Habit* (reviewed in week nineteen).

Now, on to this week's book, Jack Bickham's *Elements of Fiction Writing—Scene & Structure*. Bickham has one idea in this book, but it's a good one: cause and effect is the engine of every novel, powering both character development and plot. We've seen this point before; it's a key element of Lisa Cron's *Wired for Story* (week four), among others.

Bickham's book, however, will be of interest to authors of the action genres—especially suspense, thrillers, and mysteries—because his discussion is oriented around them. He even provides a sample "master plot" for a suspense novel, which could be a useful starting point for a pantser who wants to explore plotting and would like to work from a template. As Bickham points out, "Structure is a process, not a rigid format. Structure in fiction is not static, but dynamic." Starting from a template can insulate you from the cold terror of the blank page while also providing plenty of freedom for shape building.

While I think Cron does a better job of explaining the deep psychological roots of our attraction to cause and effect, I think Bickham adds to the discussion by exploring how cause and effect plays out on the page in what he calls "scene and sequel." Scene is what it sounds like: an action, a stimulus, an event, a character walking onto the page with a goal. The character's response to the scene is the sequel; the subsequent reaction vaults the character (and reader) into another scene. Picture a line of dominoes—when you knock over your first story event, the scene–sequel–scene chain reaction keeps your plot moving forward until the last domino falls.

Pick up a favorite book and explore how the author uses this dynamic. The beginning of Tomi Adeyemi's *Children of Blood and Bone* immediately came to mind for me. In the novel's opening sequence, the protagonist, Zélie, is plunged into a series of events and inevitable reactions—new taxes on the outcast divîners, the loss of her father's boat, her deep-seated guilt—that put her on a new path leading directly into the heart of a conflict much bigger than her immediate challenges.

What I think Bickham does so well in this book is to identify the sequel part of the equation as a space of special freedom for the writer. Bickham identifies three components of the sequel that build a bridge from one scene to another: emotion, thought, and decision. However, authors can compress, expand, or rearrange any of these at will because readers will fill in the gaps, especially later in the story when they are more familiar with your character's psychology. This is the place for synecdoche and metonymy, for letting a telling gesture stand in for an emotion, or for playing with metaphor and simile to explore a character's reactions. Experiment with interrupting the sequel with an unexpected new scene, or use it to layer in a flashback.

The sequel is also a place where a writer can use narrative summary to play with time. (For more on narrative summary, see weeks twenty and twenty-one.) Two scenes might be connected by a simple transition that jumps over weeks of time, leaving the gap cloaked in darkness or using narrative summary to pick out a few revealing details. Or the transition point might be drawn out as the character internalizes the preceding scene. Perhaps the most famous example of this last possibility is chapter 42 of Henry James's *Portrait of a Lady*, in which Isabel Archer meditates on a momentary interaction she has just glimpsed between her husband and his longtime friend. This scene is a pivot point for Isabel because she must go forward with new knowledge about herself and the other important figures in her life.

The possibilities are endless—and that's where your creativity and artistry come into play. How are you going to tell us the story of a character coming to terms with their real identity, the story of two people falling in love, the story of a character stepping up to save their community? Your brain and your experiences will suggest causes and effects we haven't seen before, connected in new ways. Novels are less like a line of dominoes and more like a Rube Goldberg machine. Get into your writing lab and start tinkering.

WEEK 37
ELIZABETH GEORGE, WRITE AWAY

It is week thirty-seven. I could almost feel a current of creative energy in the air this week as I talked to authors. People are getting back to work, and the ideas are sparking.

In last week's essay, I noted that Rube Goldberg machines are a wonderful visual metaphor for novels. A few days ago, I spotted something even better: an intricate, interlocking wooden marble run filled with dozens of marbles journeying through inventive lifts, sudden spiraling chutes, and vertiginous drops. Picture each marble as a reader being carried through the cause-and-effect machine of your novel, with every scene providing the necessary momentum to keep the reader in motion.

The marble run is a perfect metaphor for what Elizabeth George, author of this week's book, *Write Away: One Writer's Approach to the Novel*, achieves in her intricately plotted Inspector Lynley novels. They are deliberate, painstaking constructions underpinned by rich psychological portraits that provide an array of propulsive forces to keep the plot, and the reader, rolling along. In *Write Away*, George explains the process she uses to craft these plot machines.

It's no surprise to find that every novel, for her, begins with character creation. George has a "character prompt sheet," included in the book, of possible character aspects to explore and does stream-of-consciousness freewriting to build a portrait of each character. George tells us she becomes "the character's psychiatrist, psychoanalyst, probation officer, and biographer" because this allows her to "dissolve the boundaries between herself and her creations."

After completing her character profiles and researching the settings she will need, George writes a "step outline"—a basic list of scenes that she carries as far forward in the novel as she can, usually between ten to fifteen scenes. This step outline then inspires a more detailed plot outline, written, as with her character portraits, in present tense in stream-of-consciousness style. George explains that she is "strongly left-brained" and that this kind of fast-paced freewriting helps her unlock her creative right brain. She includes an example of both the step outline and the stream-of-consciousness plot outline in the book; both of them show her working out her ideas in real time, discarding and reconsidering and building as she goes.

Here, for example, is a plot outline for a scene from her 1996 novel *In the Presence of the Enemy*:

> WEDNESDAY SCENE ONE We are in Charlotte Bowen's head. It's dark because the windmill windows are boarded over and because she is on the ground floor where there are no windows at all. She comes to, out of a drugged sleep. We begin with: This is what she remembered. Or, When Charlotte Bowen lifted her head from the damp hard surface that served as her pillow, this is what she remembered. Or: Charlotte Bowen—called Lottie by her friends and Elle by her mother and Hedge by her stepfather and Tick by the people who wished she wasn't quite so persistent and irritating a

presence—opened her eyes to the darkness. (too convoluted).

After writing the plot outline, George begins drafting. When the rough draft is finished, George does what she calls a "fast read" of the whole manuscript over the course of two days and writes up an editorial letter for herself, noting weak areas to be fixed in the next draft. After that, the manuscript goes to a cold reader for feedback, which leads to a third draft if necessary.

George's process is very much aligned with the advice of Lisa Cron in *Wired for Story*, and *Write Away* would make a good companion volume to that book for any writer interested in developing a process with a great deal of preliminary plotting. If you are a confirmed pantser, this book will be less useful for you, though there are some other gems I can point you to:

- When developing characters, George identifies each one's "core need," a concept we've seen before. However, George also identifies what she calls the character's "pathological maneuver," which is the action the character takes under stress and is usually the "flip side" of the core need. As she points out, the "supreme stress" is being thwarted in the effort to fulfill the core need.
- George notes that authors should not use an omniscient narrator as "an excuse for an undisciplined sliding in and out of different characters' points of view." An author who chooses this viewpoint should have something important to say about characters, theme, setting, and so on and—most importantly—must develop a

distinctive, identifiable storyteller's voice for the narrator.
- George has a wonderful mnemonic for the background activities that can be layered behind dialogue scenes: THADs, or Talking Head Avoidance Devices. As she notes, an activity "eliminates the possibility that a scene will become nothing more than two or three talking heads; chosen wisely, it reveals character; it may in and of itself contain important information; it can be used as a metaphor."

Write Away is, to this reader at least, an easy book to learn from but a difficult book to love. It's deliberate, didactic, sometimes cranky and scolding ("finding a copy editor who knows one kind of sentence from the other these days is becoming nothing short of miraculous," George huffs). George includes painfully earnest excerpts from her writing diaries and drops in odd autobiographical details—for example, that she feels compelled to bring "a cooler of food" with her when she visits her spontaneity-loving sister-in-law lest she miss a mealtime. In addition to her very useful summary of her own process, samples of the work products of various stages, and materials like her character prompt sheet, George includes hilariously random lists of "where people work" ("drive-through dairy," "Friends of the Sea Lion," "crack house," "stained glass manufacturer") and potential Talking Head Avoidance Devices ("programming a VCR," "rowing," "robbing a liquor store," "autopsy," "figuring out Xerox," "getting a bee into a jar").

Despite these quirks, *Write Away* is worth the time for anyone interested in writing character-driven fiction, especially if you also wish to create a process for your writing that involves more planning and less spontaneous discovery. As George emphasizes, every writer must create the process that works for them: "There are no rules; there are only informed choices. But you can't make an informed choice if you remain uninformed."

WEEK 38
WALTER MOSLEY, ELEMENTS OF FICTION

It is week thirty-eight. I was thrilled this week to see that Marlon James's epic fantasy novel *Black Leopard, Red Wolf* was on the longlist for the National Book Awards for fiction. As the announcement in the *New Yorker* noted, its presence on the list, alongside Helen Phillips's twisty thriller *The Need*, signals a mixing and merging of the worlds of literary fiction and genre fiction. Tracing the division between these two worlds—and noting the ways in which the division limits authors' creative options—has been a recurring theme in my essays this year, and I'm excited to see evidence that the lines might be blurring.

Walter Mosley, author of this week's book, *Elements of Fiction*, is one writer who has given himself permission to jump around among genres and blur the line between literary and genre fiction. He's best known for his hard-boiled crime series featuring detective Easy Rawlins, but he's also written plays, nonfiction, sci-fi, and literary fiction. As a title, *Elements of Fiction* implies a kind of structural analysis of the topic that Mosley doesn't provide. Instead, Mosley skips around from character to point of view to the act of writing, dropping gems of wisdom amid sample story swatches he creates to illustrate his points. It's a confident, encouraging, optimistic book—one to reach for when you are struggling to shed your Suffocating Rubber Clown Suit of Negativity (week thirty-five) or being trampled by fear pigs (week nineteen).

The message Mosley returns to again and again is that fiction is magical: "Fiction is one of the few constructive human activities in which we have the potential to make something from almost nothing. Something from nothing. That kind of alchemy is a recipe for failure and also the hope for the miraculous." Novelists can place readers in a familiar setting—"a street-corner bodega or a country road"—and suddenly "jolt us with strange revelations: guilt that we've never experienced or an interpretation of the ordinary that stands everything we've ever believed on its head."

Fiction might be magic, but that doesn't mean writers can conjure it with a breezy snap of the fingers, like a rabbit from a hat. As Mosley admits, ushering a cast of characters with believable "passions, beliefs, scars, and successes" through the "obstacle course of story" when your only tools are "language and a smattering of punctuation" is a daunting task.

His best advice for facing the terror of the blank page—which is not a small fear, calling up as it does "the basic fear of all creatures, that of nothingness, unknowing, death"—is to approach it with a child's "wonder and a sense of play." See your keyboard, screen, pencil, and paper as toys. Imagine that blank page as "a big blue pond at dawn. All we have to do is jump in and flail around, laughing and discovering."

Elements of Fiction probably isn't going to help you decide whether your story should be told in first person, third person, or omniscient point of view or guide you through the steps required to construct a solid plot. But it's full of wisdom and joy and optimism. Mosley believes in your "acumen and imagination." He believes in your readers' willingness to participate in the "creation of the world of your story." He believes that the story—your story—"is going to be a rarefied experience." He believes that your work is important, that "a novel is the ideal of flawed, floundering, and yet heroic humanity."

I believe these things too. I believe in you. I believe that the time you spend playing with words and punctuation in that chilly blue pond at dawn is worthwhile—for yourself and, eventually, for us, your readers.

WEEK 39
STEVEN PINKER, THE SENSE OF STYLE

It is week thirty-nine. My schedule has been off-kilter this week (for good reasons this time, not pneumonia!), and I've been writing and working in a lot of new spots. My wrists have missed my split keyboard and vertical mouse, but otherwise the change has given me a welcome jolt of energy. Having a regular schedule that incorporates time for writing is important, and I think it's also true that you can train your brain to be productive at specific times (my brain starts tinkering away at these essays on Friday mornings, whether or not I'm sitting at my keyboard). But it's also true that occasionally shuffling your routine can wake you up.

I also, just by happenstance, read this week's book—Steven Pinker's *The Sense of Style: The Thinking Person's Guide to Writing in the 21st Century*—in a different format than I usually do. As much as I love print books (and I still buy and borrow plenty of them), I prefer reading my weekly craft books on my Kindle e-reader so I can easily reference my notes or search the books from my computer.

However, I happened to buy *The Sense of Style* on Apple Books soon after it came out in 2014, so I reread it on my iPad, which turned out to have some advantages. The layout of the book is stylish, and that's something that often gets lost on an e-reader. Pinker also includes a number of cartoons and, more importantly, sentence diagrams and other visuals, and these come across much better on iPad than on my Kindle Paperwhite. (I haven't tried it, but I'm guessing the experience on a Kindle Fire or the Kindle app for PC or iOS is similar to Apple Books.) On the other hand, it's much harder to get my highlights and notes out of Apple Books and into my note-taking program. The iPad is also much heavier and clunkier than my Kindle.

If you are an indie author who self-publishes, it's worth making the effort to try out various devices so you can understand what your readers' experience is likely to be. I use Vellum for formatting and appreciate how easily you can see the layout in different e-readers, but it's not a substitute for holding a device in your hand and reading from it.

Now, on to Pinker's book, which is full of gems however you happen to experience it. For fiction writers, Pinker's book doesn't supersede my recommendation of Brian Shawver's *Language of Fiction*, but *Sense of Style* will be appreciated by anyone who writes nonfiction as well as fiction and by writers who want to know the logic behind the rules. A psycholinguist and cognitive scientist, Pinker always brings us back to the *why*, not just the *what* and the *how*. As he puts it, "The rules often mash together issues of grammatical correctness, logical coherence, formal style, and standard dialect, but a skilled writer needs to keep them straight."

Pinker also does an excellent job of distinguishing between current usage and outdated "rules." One stated goal of the book is to give writers "the ability to discriminate between the principles that improve the quality of prose and the superstitions, fetishes, shibboleths, and initiation ordeals that have been passed down in the traditions of usage."

Remember this when someone in a writing group tells you to take every -ly word out of your manuscript. Rather than immediately firing up the "find" command in Word, spend some time figuring out the logic behind the recommendation. *The Sense of Style* would be a good place to start.

Pinker starts the book by taking apart some sample passages of excellent prose and "reverse-engineering" them to find out how they work, a practice he returns to throughout the book. As he reminds us, "Good writers are avid readers," and their skills often come not from stylebooks but from reading excellent writing.

In this first chapter, Pinker identifies a few hallmarks of good writing:

- Find fresh wording: for example, even when a cliché is the best way to convey an idea, a good writer can make it new. Original: "Trying to direct team owners is like herding cats." Revised: "To suggest that directing team owners is like herding cats is to give cats a bad name."
- Avoid "verbal coffins": rather than leaning on abstract nouns and nominalizations, direct the reader's gaze to a concrete thing or "telling detail" that can stand in for an abstraction.
- Vary your prose: mix repeating patterns (like parallel syntax) and familiar nouns with an occasional "planned surprise," like an unusual word or a jump cut using a colon or dash.
- Model conversation: a successful piece of writing "directs the reader's gaze to something in the world."

Writers interested in grammar and the deep structure of language will enjoy chapter 4, evocatively titled "The Web, the String, and the Tree." As Pinker explains the metaphor, these are "the three things that grammar brings together: the web of ideas in our head, the string of words that comes out of our mouth or fingers, and the tree of syntax that converts the first into the second." This chapter is largely concerned with the tree, and Pinker explores the ways different kinds of words function in sentences and how, as both readers and writers, our brains work to group words and ideas into clusters to produce meaning. As a writer, you don't necessarily need to wrestle with this chapter. But Pinker points out, "Learning how to bring the units of language into consciousness can allow a writer to reason his way to a grammatically consistent sentence when his intuitions fail him, and to diagnose the problem when he knows something is wrong with the sentence but can't put his finger on what it is." (Interestingly, Pinker is a proponent of "singular they" when he directly addresses the topic but has chosen to use the alternating genders approach in this book.)

Chapter 6, "Telling Right from Wrong," is itself worth the price of the book. It's prefaced with a reasoned discussion of what constitutes an error and how to make judicious decisions about what is right for your book and your readers. What follows is an alphabetically arranged list of common grammatical quandaries that you can turn to when someone tells you, for instance, that your work is full of dangling modifiers. (Here's an example of a problematic dangler: "As a baboon who grew up wild in the jungle, I realized that Wiki had special nutritional needs." And here's a dangler you can let pass since it won't trip up the reader: "Considering the hour, it is surprising that he arrived at all.")

Throughout the book, Pinker insists on the transformational power of writing. "Good writing," Pinker says, "can flip the way the world is perceived, like the silhouette in psychology textbooks which oscillates between a goblet and two faces." This is true not just for readers but also for writers. Participating in that imagined conversation with the reader forces writers to escape the "curse of knowledge," which leads to false assumptions about what a reader already knows and understands, and instead to find fresh ways to climb the tree of syntax and transfer a web of ideas from one mind to another.

WEEK 40
JOHN GARDNER, THE ART OF FICTION

It's week forty. How was the writing this week? It's October now—the true heart of Fuck It Fall—and now is the time to push yourself creatively just a bit. What can you begin or accomplish in the handful of weeks left in the year? Set a stop date for yourself, then start sprinting. Knowing that the sprint won't last forever can help you stick with it when it gets hard.

It took all my resolve to push myself to the end of this week's book, John Gardner's *The Art of Fiction: Notes on Craft for Young Writers*. I carted around a paperback copy of this book for many years (far past the time I would generally be accounted "young"), always intending to read it but never getting past the first chapter or so. Until this week, I had never thought about why; I just attributed it to the same failure of will and persistence that led me to abandon novel manuscripts after a few chapters.

This time through, I immediately identified why I kept drifting away from this book. Gardner's imagined writer, in addition to being young, is also male. The first words of the book tell us that "this is a book designed to teach the serious beginning writer the art of fiction. I assume from the outset that the would-be writer using this book can become a successful writer if he wants to, since most of the people I've known who wanted to become writers, knowing what it meant, did become writers. About all that is required is that the would-be writer understand clearly what it is that he wants to become and what he must do to become it." This is the so-called "universal he," of course, which was ubiquitous in 1983, when the book was first published, but the steady drumbeat of *he, he, he* required by Gardner's frequent references to an unspecified, generic writer are difficult to ignore, especially for a twenty-first-century reader for whom this usage is (thankfully!) no longer familiar. Gardner reassures us, though not until almost halfway through the book, that "this book speaks of the writer as 'he,' though many of the best writers I have read or have taught in writing classes are female" but doesn't feel compelled to change his pronouns, breezily dismissing the problem by remarking that "English, like most languages, is covertly male chauvinist." In another passage, he tells us that "art produces the most important progress civilization knows," noting in wonderment that "the age-old idea of human dignity comes to apply even to the indigent, even to slaves, even to immigrants, now recently even to women."

The problem is compounded by Gardner's almost complete inability to see women as creators as well as subjects of fiction. In a book packed with references to specific authors, only a tiny handful are women, none of whom receive more than a bare mention. His fictional examples are full of problematic portrayals of figures like an "intelligent middle-aged housewife . . . who has read about women's liberation in her magazines and feels an increasingly anxious inclination . . . to take a nightschool course—one in flower-arranging, or ceramics, or self-awareness" or an aging but "well-preserved" stripper of thirty-six who flies into a rage and hits a construction worker with her car when her highly choreographed act ("she has, let us say, trained white doves who fly away with each article of clothing she takes off") loses its top billing, replaced by younger strippers who "take off their clothes as indifferently as trees drop leaves." The writer might, Gardner muses, center this particular story on the theme of nakedness; hence, "he finds himself bringing in black strippers, perhaps an Indian stripper, supported by imagery that recalls primitive nakedness." (My notes on this book are littered with WTFs.)

Gardner also has the off-putting tendency to see failures in technique as evidence of moral or intellectual weakness. Writing is often described with anthropomorphic adjectives like "cloddish," "clumsy," or "awkward." "Diction problems," Gardner tells us, presumably with a sad shake of the head, "are usually symptomatic of defects in the character or education of the writer. Both diction shifts and the steady use of inappropriate diction suggest either deep-down bad taste or the awkwardness that comes of inexperience and timidity. There seems little or no hope for the adult writer who produces sentences like these." Even worse are what Gardner terms "faults of soul": sentimentality, frigidity, and mannerism. A frigid writer "lacks the kind of passion all true artists possess. He lacks the nobility of spirit that enables a real writer to enter deeply into the feelings of imaginary characters."

Gardner makes it clear that his book is "not for the writer of nurse books or thrillers or porno or the cheaper sort of sci-fi" but "for serious literary artists," though he concedes that "most creative-writing teachers have had the experience of occasionally helping to produce, by accident, a pornographer. The most elegant techniques in the world, filtered through a junk mind, become elegant junk techniques."

Now, for those elect readers still left, the "true artists," Gardner provides a rather terrifying analogy: "Circus knife-throwers know that it is indeed possible to be perfect, and one had better be. Perfection means hitting exactly what you are aiming at and not touching by a hair what you are not." *The Art of Fiction* provides some "warnings" and "hints" about how to avoid killing one's subject by a knife in the forehead and then closes with suggested exercises that range from the hopelessly general ("18. Plot a novel") to the ridiculously specific ("24. Without an instant's lapse of taste, describe a person [a] going to the bathroom, [b] vomiting, [c] murdering a child").

I can, however, point to four nuggets of wisdom that might be valuable to any writer—even you pornographers. First is Gardner's deservedly well-known description of fiction as a "vivid and continuous dream" for readers. The writer's goal is to avoid disrupting the dream by any false note (unless that happens to be your intent, you amoral metafictionist). This is a good metaphor to keep in mind when you feel stuck in an endless loop of revision and editing. You are doing this hard labor so that your eventual reader remains enchanted in the fictional dream you have conjured for them.

Second, Gardner makes the point that the novel, like a symphony, can make good use of repetition to enhance meaning and, especially, to achieve a "resonant close." He advises writers to read their work over again and again, "watching for subtle meanings, connections, accidental repetitions, psychological significance" and then nudging these elements closer to the surface to catch the reader's attention. (But be tasteful about it! I'm looking at you, writers of porno nurse thrillers.)

Third, Gardner notes that writers should be wary of "filter words" that put the veil of the character's consciousness between the reader and the thing described. Compare these two examples:

- "Turning, she noticed two snakes fighting in among the rocks."
- "She turned. In among the rocks, two snakes were fighting."

Unless the fact of the character noticing or seeing is important (and sometimes it is), give us an unmediated description of your subject. (Especially if it is a dove carrying away an item of a "well-preserved" stripper's clothing.)

Lastly, Gardner provides a very useful example of the range of effects you can achieve through altering "the distance the reader feels between himself and the events in the story." The following passage gradually reduces the psychic distance until, in the final sentence, the reader gets subsumed in the narrative "you": "It was winter of the year 1853. A large man stepped out of a doorway. Henry J. Warburton had never much cared for snowstorms. Henry hated snowstorms. God how he hated these damn snowstorms. Snow. Under your collar, down inside your shoes, freezing and plugging up your miserable soul." (Methinks poor Henry needs to go back inside and curl up with a nice nurse porno thriller, no?)

Gardner would likely scorn the comparison, but it strikes me that writing craft books have a great deal in common with the larger category of self-help books. Self-help writers know that they must immediately establish a rapport with their readers—show them that they are seen and understood and welcomed with all of their flaws. I ended up with *The Art of Fiction* on my bookshelf in part because there weren't very many writing craft books available in the early nineties, and this was likely the one I found on a bookstore shelf and bought. This year of reading has shown me—and you, dear readers—that there are books out there for all of us (even nurse porno thriller writers!). Find your way to the books that are congenial to you—those are the ones you will learn from.

WEEK 41
MEREDITH MARAN, WHY WE WRITE

It's week forty-one. I've been thinking a lot about choices this week. It's the time of year in San Francisco when there are simply too many good things happening at once: the Hardly Strictly Bluegrass festival in Golden Gate Park, the best camping weather of the year, LitQuake readings and book discussions, a great new play at ACT, some of my favorite bands at the Fillmore and the Fox. And then next month, there's the perennial NaNoWriMo versus Thanksgiving showdown.

I realized this week that I was letting my regret at the things I will miss contaminate my joy in the things I do get to do. (Not to mention: how fabulously lucky am I to have this banquet of choices laid out in front of me?) So if right now is not your season for writing, don't let my frequent question get you down. Last week, I counseled you to have a stop date for your sprint if you are doing one. Similarly, this week, I'm telling you to have a tentative start date to begin if you aren't writing. Put that date in your mind and on your calendar and then focus your joy and attention on those things you are doing right now.

On to this week's book, *Why We Write: 20 Acclaimed Authors on How and Why They Do What They Do*, edited by Meredith Maran. The writers profiled in this book are nothing if not idiosyncratic in their approaches to writing, and they are far enough along in their careers to convey confidence in their choices.

Sarah Gruen confesses that before starting each book, she arranges a collection of colorful rocks inside a golden horseshoe and then doesn't touch them until the book is done. James Frey looks at a magazine cover of boxer Marvin Hagler with the headline "The Best and the Baddest" to remind himself of what he wants to be. (This is James Frey the author of *A Million Little Pieces*, not James Frey the mystery writer, whose book I reviewed in week twenty-one. Frey was the only writer in the collection to earn a WTF from me this week, for his confession that he wrote "a big, corny, DreamWorks teenage action movie" under a pen name. Apparently it didn't fit in with his avowed goal to be "the most widely read, most controversial, most influential writer" of his time.)

Ann Patchett still writes in WordPerfect (which I didn't even know was possible). Mary Karr writes longhand due to repetitive stress injuries. Michael Lewis's palms sweat so much when he writes that his keyboard gets wet. (Lewis also tells us that he happened to be living next door to Judi Dench when his first book was published. She told him, "When your book comes, just drop it on the floor and listen to the sound it makes." He followed her instructions, Lewis reports, "and it was just great.") Terry McMillan fills out a McDonald's employment application for each of her characters and uses an astrology book to determine their birthdays. Susan Orlean needs a room of her own in which to write so she can "put things on the wall that don't require approval from anyone else" and leave her "notes laid out in a certain way

ALL THE WORDS

and know they'll be exactly that way" when she returns. ("Your publisher," Orlean also warns us, "is a frenemy in the most pure sense. You pretend you're on the same team but in many ways, you're not.")

The steady *I, I, I* of this book was the perfect antidote to the *he, he, he* of last week's book, John Gardner's *The Art of Fiction*. It's not a book that will teach you much about how to write, but it's a book that will remind you that writers—even famous, successful ones—are people just like you, with weird anxieties and secret desires and unreasonable enmities.

Why We Write will also remind you that writing can help us make sense of our strange world and the people who inhabit it. Kathryn Harrison says, "I write . . . because it's the apparatus I have for explaining the world around me, seemingly the only method that works." Writing provides a place of control. As Meg Wolitzer puts it, "You can't control other people or your relationships or your children, but in writing you can have sustained periods where you're absolutely in charge." Rick Moody calls the blank page "a peaceful and cloistered space . . . where I don't feel pressured the way I do in the world."

And you have free access to this control, to this peaceful space. Walter Mosley says, "If you're looking to get married, you need another person. If you're looking to write, you really don't." Words, Isabel Allende reminds us gleefully, are free: "No matter how many syllables they have: free! You can use as many as you want, forever." You just have to choose the ones you want.

WEEK 42
JESSICA MORRELL, THANKS, BUT THIS ISN'T FOR US

It's week forty-two. I put in a lot of editing hours this week, bookended by a quick camping trip to Salt Point State Park—which has the stunning Northern California combination of pine forests and dramatic beaches, along with a restful lack of cell phone signal—and a concert by the talented J. S. Ondara, a Kenyan folk singer whose music brought a packed and rowdy club to hushed silence. In other words, it was a pretty perfect week.

Another pleasure of this perfect week was keeping company with Jessica Morrell in her bracingly honest and instructive book, *Thanks, but This Isn't for Us: A (Sort of) Compassionate Guide to Why Your Writing Is Being Rejected*. The back cover copy claims this book is "fun," which, in addition to being inaccurate, is an example of the kind of bland generality Morrell would root out with her scalpel-sharp red pen.

If you are the faint-hearted sort or prone to self-doubt, then this book might not be for you. Morrell admits in her acknowledgments that her book is "filled with smack talk and that I'm letting out the smart-ass, bitchy, and opinionated editor within." She has no qualms about drawing lessons from problem manuscripts (and even a couple problem clients) she's encountered in her years of editing, confessing, "I've ... read manuscripts by writers who can barely manage to string together sentences, and some who are clearly a few sandwiches short of a picnic." It's possible that her frequent expressions of exasperation (flinging manuscripts across the room, groans of despair, the need for a stiff drink) may stoke any fears you already have about working with an editor.

Thanks, but This Isn't for Us may not be "fun," but it is darkly funny. Morrell is entertaining in her exasperation ("don't even get me started on how some writers become miffed when I suggest that stream-of-consciousness journal entries do not a memoir make; that paragraphs shouldn't occupy four pages; or that you cannot stick bizarre punctuation onto each page as if scattering rose petals before a bride"), and her labels for common problems are memorable and effective warnings. Who wants to have their cherished manuscript stuck with the label "All Hat, No Cattle" or (my favorite) "Faulkneresque, or Someone Left a Cake out in the Rain"? *Not you* is the answer.

Morrell is right that "while all great writing is unique, all bad writing shares common traits," and her goal in this book is to warn you away from those mistakes. As she says, "Tough critiquing is a basic and essential part of the writing process. It's not only a fact that beginning writers need to accept; it's likely the only way your writing will improve." Amen.

Each chapter starts with a solid explanation of the topic at hand. In chapter 2, for example, Morrell gives a succinct overview of story structure and provides brief "blueprints" of different kinds (chronological, nonlinear, frame, etc.). After her overview, Morrell offers a list of "Deal Breakers"—common problems afflicting manuscripts—and then a list of effective strategies to consider. Each chapter ends with a "Try This" exercise to help writers practice a specific skill and a list of "Quick and Dirty Tips" that summarize the lessons of the chapter and provide additional advice.

If you have gotten vague feedback from beta readers, agents, or publishers, Morrell's book will help you identify what is wrong with your manuscript and understand how to fix it. A few useful gems:

- "Think about the external conflict as the dragon in the story because this reminds us that it can be seen, heard, and felt, while internal conflict—your character's emotional and psychological struggles, or inner conflict—can be called the demon."
- "Dialogue is never a copy of real-life speech—it's more like conversation's greatest hits. It's always crisper, punchier, and embedded with subtext—the sea of emotions that runs beneath a scene but is never spoken out loud."
- "Scenes are mini-containers for drama, the events where your characters go to work just as actors show up on a stage."
- "Remember, adjectives tell and verbs show. For example, instead of shiny necklace, trade the adjective shiny for a verb: the necklace glinted or the necklace sparkled, gleamed, flashed, glimmered, shimmered, twinkled."

Perhaps my favorite bit of advice in the whole book is this: "Reading is your job. If you don't read the genre you're writing in, your unconscious will never absorb the techniques and structure needed." Morrell recounts a writing workshop she once taught in which not a single participant had read twenty books in their genre. I'm convinced that constant reading is the secret sauce of all great writers. And it's something you can do to improve your work even when you are stuck or between projects or too busy to start the writing itself.

Reading *Thanks, but This Isn't for Us* may make you feel like a hypochondriac reading a diagnostic manual, but I think it's worth the possible pain. If you can learn to spot and correct the weaknesses in your story, you will be your own best editor. An editor can wield a scalpel, but it is ultimately the writer who must then stitch up the gaps or grow a whole new limb through the magical power of creativity.

WEEK 43

CHARLES JOHNSON, THE WAY OF THE WRITER

It is week forty-three. How is the writing going? I was working on an edit of a cli-fi novel this week while monitoring air quality predictions to see if my kids' schools would close due to wildfire smoke, as has happened here the previous two falls. It was a reminder to me—and now to you—that stories matter. Writers, you are some of our most important truth tellers, and the work you are doing can change lives. You don't have to be writing on a newsy topic either—all successful novels help us become better humans, whether we're wrestling with big societal problems or negotiating personal relationships. Remember this the next time you feel guilty about the time you spend on your writing.

Charles Johnson, author of this week's book, *The Way of the Writer: Reflections on the Art and Craft of Storytelling*, would agree with me on this. As you'll see, we diverge in our thinking on a number of other topics. When I chose this book, I knew that Johnson is the author of National Book Award–winning *Middle Passage*—a searing account of the slave trade that uses eighteenth-century story forms in fresh ways—and that he had been a university writing teacher for decades. What I didn't know but quickly discovered is that one of Johnson's key mentors was our old friend John Gardner (see week forty), whom Johnson references so often that he just shortens his name to JG. One bookshelf in his office, Johnson tells us, "contains every scholarly book and work of fiction JG published."

(The portrait of "JG" that emerges in Johnson's book didn't make me like him any better. Take this passage: "I remember when he was going over one of my chapters for *Faith* in his office at Southern Illinois University and I asked if he needed to stop in order to prepare for his creative-writing workshop. Gardner shook his mane of silver hair and said, 'No, teaching creative writing is a joke,' and we continued with his critique of my work until the bell rang for him to go to class." WTF, right? Here's another: "He said he gave a reading, and during the Q&A a woman raised her hand and said, 'You know, I think I like your writing, but I don't think I like you.' His reply was memorable. 'That's all right,' he said, 'because I'm a better person when I'm writing.'" According to Johnson, Gardner saw this as a story about the power of revision—that it gave writers time to consider and correct their words. What's missing from the story is what it was that compelled this woman to raise her hand and, in front of the assembled audience, tell the man on stage she didn't like him.)

If you couldn't tell by now, I struggled through this book. What I had hoped to find was a distillation of the curriculum Johnson used with his students. What I got instead was a collection of musings that Johnson tells us were carved out from "the 672-page tome *The Words and Wisdom of Charles Johnson*," published in 2015 and based on a year of email correspondence with poet E. Ethelbert Miller.

Now, there's a place for writing books that take you on a meandering tour of a writer's mind and habits. Many of my favorite books about writing—including Anne Lamott's *Bird by Bird* and Walter Mosley's *Elements of Fiction*—follow this format. We wander through the landscape of the writer's thoughts, discovering helpful bons mots along the path. But you have to enjoy being in the landscape of that author's mind for it to work.

The landscape Johnson presents is likely congenial to some readers, but not to this one. In addition to his devotion to "JG," Johnson has the off-putting habit of quoting from literary scholar Marc Connor, who has published books on Johnson's work; he makes the tiresome complaint that 1980s identity politics caused his students to create work that was "depressingly less imaginative and daring, but more politically correct"; he disapproves of swearing, bemoaning the "coarseness, vulgarity, and at times obscenity that we encounter so often today in American speech" (WTF, right?); and he confesses that he "broods daily about the debasement of American speech" (to which I say, read Gretchen McCulloch's brilliant *Because Internet* and heal thyself).

The class Johnson formulated for his creative-writing students does sound like it was a good one: "I felt it should be a labor-intensive 'skill acquisition' course, emphasizing the sequential acquisition of fiction techniques and providing the opportunity to practice them. The curriculum should be capacious, allowing for instruction in all styles, genres, and subgenres of fiction." He gave lectures "on plot, description, dialogue, character, the structure of dramatic scenes, and so forth" and provided students with "a checklist of twenty-four crucial questions they should ask in regard to fiction, not merely in terms of 'themes' but about how a document is made, the decisions that went into its construction, and whether those were the best choices for fulfilling the writer's intention." Frustratingly, none of this material has made it into *The Way of the Writer*. (He also tells this story: "In my classes I constantly emphasized the virtues I believed great writers brought to their creations. After one such mini-lecture twenty-five years ago that had me huffing and puffing for perhaps twenty minutes, a young woman raised her hand and said, 'You know, I'm glad you told us that.' I asked her why. Her reply was, 'Because now I understand that I don't want to be a great writer. I just want to write a few stories and maybe get them published, and that's all.'" I hope she published her stories, then a few more, then maybe several novels.)

There were some bits and pieces of this book I enjoyed. For instance, Johnson tells us that some of his early reading material came by way of his mother's occasional second job cleaning the Gamma Phi Beta sorority house at Northwestern University: "My mother brought home boxes of books thrown out by the sorority girls when classes ended, and in those boxes I found my first copies of Mary Shelley and Shakespeare. I read them, determined that the privileged girls of that sorority would never be able to say they knew something about the Bard that the son of their holiday cleaning woman didn't." His mother told him that the sorority had declared they would never admit black or Jewish students. Decades later, Johnson, who is African American, was offered a position as chair in the humanities at the university.

A lover of long sentences myself, I also enjoyed Johnson's extravagant prose and his discussion of sentence length:

> If I don't control myself, my sentences in literary fiction naturally tend to run long, with image and idea building upon image and idea, rolling and ribboning out, sometimes twisting and torquing dialectically, from thesis to antithesis, and spiced with colons and semicolons and parenthetical asides (such as this) until I simply can't pack any more into

> them. I've always seen the sentence and paragraph as units of energy to be released. So yes, I use long sentences for rhythm and music. I most certainly would always follow one with a short sentence.

Johnson is a master of the technique, on full display in *Middle Passage*. We'll learn more about it in week forty-six and week forty-nine, when I review Virginia Tufte's *Artful Sentences* and Brooks Landon's *Building Great Sentences*.

Johnson reminds us that "art should always be a form of play" and tells us that, when tasked with evaluating a pile of three hundred books to be considered for a major literary prize, "what I do is try for a moment to forget absolutely everything I've learned about literature in the last fifty years. . . . [When] I begin looking through those books, what I'm hungering for is the same innocent enchantment I had when I was a reader of twelve or thirteen. . . . In the midst of this enchantment, I didn't want to stop reading or go to bed or do anything else until I'd learned how events in the story unfolded, because I was certain the outcome had meaning for my own life." Those are the readers you are writing for: the ones who open your book believing that your words have meaning for them. As Johnson says, "To imagine things differently is the first step in changing the world as it is given to us. It is, in fact, the first step toward freedom." Whatever genre you are writing in, this power is yours.

WEEK 44
DONALD MAAS, WRITING THE BREAKOUT NOVEL

It is week forty-four. Are you participating in NaNoWriMo (National Novel Writing Month) this year? It's not too late to start, even if you have only a germ of an idea. Completing ten or twenty thousand words of exploratory writing can be enough to understand your characters and feel your way toward a plot or a theme, at which point you can step back and productively plan out the rest of a draft. There's a thriving community on Twitter ready to keep you company and cheer you on.

This week's book, *Writing the Breakout Novel: Winning Advice from a Top Agent and His Best-Selling Client* by Donald Maas, is frequently cited by editors discussing knotty craft problems, and now I know why. Maas pushes past the basics on every topic he covers, delivering fresh insights about important aspects of craft.

Here are some of my favorite takeaways:

- On setting: don't focus on "how a place looks but its psychological effect on the characters in your novel"; give your characters "an active relationship

to place" by showing their "growth (or decline) through their relationships to their various surroundings."
- On character: write "larger-than-life characters" who "act in ways that are unusual, unexpected, dramatic, decisive, full of consequence and are irreversible"; breakout characters also have a "sense of self-regard. Their emotions matter to them. They do not dismiss what they experience."
- On plot: look for complex conflicts rather than clear good versus evil; "consider motivating your main characters in mixed ways. Put them in situations that are strong but in which the right path is not obvious"; remember that "the hero's journey is not a universal plot cure"—there are alternate forms that might work better for your story.
- On subplot: find nodes of connection where your subplot impacts your main plot; see if you can combine roles for secondary characters, so that they have more than one relationship with your main character.
- On voice: "To set your voice free, set your words free. Set your characters free. Most important, set your heart free. It is from the unknowable shadows of your subconscious that your stories will find their drive and from which they will draw their meaning. No one can loan you that or teach you that. Your voice is your self in the story."
- On theme: "If authentic, theme is not something apart from story but something intrinsic to it. It is not embedded, but rather emerges."

Basics are important, and writers need to learn those

first. (My recommendations if you want to start with the basics: Chuck Wendig's *Damn Fine Story*, week sixteen; Janet Burroway's *Writing Fiction*, week twenty; Lisa Cron's *Wired for Story*, week four.) But if you are a couple books into your writing career and feel like you are pushing the boundaries of what you already know, *Writing the Breakout Novel* will show you some techniques that will deepen and enrich your writing.

Writing the Breakout Novel came out in 2001, and so the framing chapters about the publishing business are dated. Likely you are not worried that your editor is going to be "bolting to a dot com," nor are you going to send your query via snail mail with an SASE. However, the craft advice, despite the predominantly mid-1990s examples, feels fresh. And there was only one WTF moment for me in this book, when Maas suggests that the dichotomy of Ashley Wilkes and Rhett Butler in *Gone with the Wind* originated in the contrast between Rochester in *Jane Eyre* and Heathcliff in *Wuthering Heights*, which makes me believe that Maas has never read *Jane Eyre*.

What I like about this book (and some others I've covered this year, like James Scott Bell's *Write Your Novel from the Middle*) is that Maas starts from a question: What sets a breakout novel apart from other novels? And then he reads books to answer his question. In one chapter, he tells us that he is writing from a hotel room, without access to his library, so he strolls down to a nearby used bookstore, spots a copy of Carson McCullers's *The Member of the Wedding* in the bargain paperback bin, and uses it as an example of how to use "bridging conflict," a tiny bit of tension, to keep readers engaged and moving forward in the story.

Writers, this strategy is open to you too! What are you struggling with? Maybe your big question is how to introduce readers to your fantasy world without drowning them in detail. Go to your shelves or go to your local library and see how other authors have solved this problem. (If you want help finding excellent exemplars in your genre, ask a librarian—they love advising on these kinds of questions.) As I've said many times in this book, I think reading constantly is one of the best (and most enjoyable) things you can do to improve your writing. But rereading—coming back to books you admire with specific questions—can teach you even more.

WEEK 45
JOHN TRUBY, THE ANATOMY OF STORY

It is week forty-five. My week has been jam-packed with stories of all sorts: a Lucinda Williams concert in which she told us the stories behind the stories of her songs; two client manuscripts with plots to be deepened and refined; a Harry Potter movie marathon in preparation for seeing the two-night theater spectacle of *The Cursed Child*; and a student performance of Thornton Wilder's *Our Town*. I have laughed and cried and counseled and plotted and marveled and shout-sung ("You took my joy; I want it back") and rolled my eyes (Wilder, WTF with the sentimental nihilism?).

I have been on some journeys this week, and each one of them has taught me again that the very best stories—the ones that hold us transfixed in time, the ones we can't shake—are those that have emotional depth. They continue to resonate for the audience and even for their creators. Lucinda Williams told a story about her father, the poet Miller Williams, listening to her perform "Car Wheels on a Gravel Road" for the first time. After the performance, he found her backstage and apologized to her. Until that moment she had not thought of the song as being about her childhood, but it was immediately clear to her that it was. The raw power of that song was fueled by an energy Williams hadn't even realized she had tapped.

That's the problem we wrestle with as writers, right? Those emotional depths where the idea fish swim are often chilly, dark places. Maybe on a Tuesday at 8:00 a.m. we don't feel inclined to jump in. Maybe we don't ever feel inclined to jump in. Maybe we don't even know yet where the shores are —maybe we are just stumbling around blindly until we fall in.

And that's the problem I struggle with when I read books like John Truby's *Anatomy of Story*. You can think all day about your one-sentence premise or your seven key story steps or your three-part character equation or your four-cornered opponents, but you aren't going to be able to construct a resonant story out of these bits and pieces until you tap into your hard-earned emotional wisdom. (I've spent a lot of time this week marveling at Rowling's dazzling variety of disenfranchised, alienated characters—from Snape to Luna Lovegood to Neville Longbottom to Harry himself— and how many routes to redemption and community she finds for them.)

Truby does know that emotional depth is a central component of all great stories. He even makes it the first step of constructing your one-sentence premise (after warning us, wide eyed, that "nine of ten writers" fail at this point in the process):

> Step 1: Write Something That May Change Your Life. This is a very high standard, but it may be the most valuable piece of advice you'll ever get as a writer. I've never seen a writer go wrong following it. Why? Because if a story is that important to you, it may be that important to a lot of people

in the audience. And when you're done writing the story, no matter what else happens, you've changed your life.

However, the problem is that many of us can't just conjure life-changing emotional depth out of thin air. We may need to write our way into it. Maybe, like Lucinda Williams, we don't even recognize we've created it until someone else points it out.

You should read Truby's book because it is full of useful tactics and insights. But you should not be frustrated if you find that you can't follow Truby's checklists and steps (so many steps!). Don't get caught up in the trap of dissecting and labelling the pieces of your story (is this the self-revelation scene or the new-equilibrium scene?). Instead, use this book as an encyclopedia of plot moves and character insights that can inspire you to keep digging deeper and show you what to do with the treasures you unearth.

WEEK 46

VIRGINIA TUFTE, ARTFUL SENTENCES

It is week forty-six. How is the writing going? I have two clients who are using NaNoWriMo energy to power their revisions, which I think is a brilliant strategy. Set your own goal for winning and then see how far it takes you. Maybe your goal is to take the first brave step of creating a file called "novel" and roughing out a character or scenario that has been kicking around in your brain for years. In a blog post called "Start Before You Think You're Ready," Austin Kleon quoted a question that the environmentalist and writer Stewart Brand asked of Brian Eno, who included it in his 1995 diary: "Why don't you assume you've written your book already—and all you have to do now is find it?"[1] Why don't you?

This week's book, Virginia Tufte's *Artful Sentences: Syntax as Style*, came to my attention in a similarly roundabout way. It was mentioned in a tweet by writer and book reviewer Mark Athitakis, who notes that Lydia Davis raves about it in her new essay collection. I've been a fan of Lydia Davis's prickly, tricky short stories for years, so Tufte's book was immediately added to my list. (Davis's essay collection is on there as well now too.)

Fun sidenote for serious book nerds: Virginia Tufte is, as it happens, the mother of Edward Tufte, whose 1983 book *The Visual Display of Quantitative Information* has the status of cult object among both data scientists and book designers. Edward Tufte's Graphics Press is publisher of *Artful Sentences*, and the book is as beautifully and clearly designed as one would expect. It's only available in print, and it was a joy to read in that format.

Artful Sentences is, as promised, a treasure trove of wisdom about sentence construction. (My favorite one-liner from the book: "Parallelism is saying like things in like ways.") There are a lot of grammar terms here, and Tufte doesn't generally stop to explain them, but it doesn't matter. (Though if you do want to tackle the grammar, turn to Brooks Landon's *Building Great Sentences*, which I review in week forty-nine.) Skip along past her references to objective complements and predicate subjects and go right to her illuminating examples, which make everything clear. (From the range and quality and number of examples, it's clear that Tufte collected them for many years.) You don't need to know what an appositive is in order to use one in your writing. You just need to imprint the structure in your brain. Read these sentences slowly, maybe copy down some of your favorites and stick them on a wall in your writing space, and make the structures your own.

Tufte's focus on syntax—the order of elements in a sentence—sets this book apart from other writing books. As she describes it, "It is the words that shine and sparkle and glitter, sometimes radiant with an author's inspired choice. But it is syntax that gives words the power to relate to each other in a sequence, to create rhythms and emphasis, to carry meaning—of whatever kind—as well as glow individually in just the right place." Tufte treats sentences like living machines that can be assembled in myriad patterns to create predictable effects. She talks about simple subject-verb clauses that act as "kernels" supporting right- or left-branching phrases. She is alert to the degree of "activity" in verbs, according to their kind and placement in a sentence. She pays attention to where the "news" of the sentence is located (usually at the end but sometimes, with careful use of inversion, at the beginning.)

This opening paragraph from Rebecca West's *The Birds Fall Down* illustrates a few of Tufte's points:

> One afternoon, in an early summer of this century, when Laura Rowan was just eighteen, she sat, embroidering a handkerchief, on the steps leading down from the terrace of her father's house to the gardens communally owned by the residents in Radnage Square. She liked embroidery.

The kernel of that long first sentence is *she sat*. This kernel is dense and straightforward; *sit* is an intransitive verb, meaning that it doesn't require an object (*require* is a transitive verb that demands an object for its action). The simple kernel can support phrases that branch off from it in both directions. As Tufte points out, the branches in West's sentence are "free modifiers," which means we can easily break them off from the core of the sentence. We lose detail if we break them off, but we don't garble the meaning altogether. Punctuation like commas and use of prepositions like *in* and *when* and *on* allow readers to mentally store these phrases in syntactical slots and thus easily understand a complex sentence like this one. Note also that West follows this long sentence with a very short one.

Using free modifiers to build complex sentences is better than using "bound modifiers," which require the reader to hold multiple phrases in suspension until they reach the end of the sentence. Compare West's sentence with this one, from Earl W. Hayter's *The Troubled Farmer*:

> Neglect of this rich mine of information is due in part to the difficulty one faces in attempting to establish a suitable model in this area for modern quantification techniques that have contributed immeasurably to the formulation of historical generalizations in such areas as economic history and voting patterns.

As Tufte points out, the problem here is the thirty-seven-word noun phrase beginning with *the difficulty*, which acts as the object of the verb *due*.

Tufte, however, rarely shows us examples of bad writing. Her joy is to unearth sentences that seem like inscrutable little miracles, and then take them apart and show us how they work—especially when they violate the "rules" of good grammar. For example, this beauty of a chapter from Sandra Cisneros's *The House on Mango Street*:

> Not a flat. Not an apartment in back. Not a man's house. Not a daddy's. A house all my own. With my porch and my pillow, my pretty purple petunias. My books and my stories. My two shoes waiting beside the bed. Nobody to shake a stick at. Nobody's garbage to pick up after.
>
> Only a house quiet as snow, a space for myself to go, clean as paper before the poem.

Tufte points out that the entire chapter consists of a series of sentence fragments, all of them built around noun phrases and all of them "in apposition to"—renaming—the chapter title, "A House of My Own."

In each chapter, Tufte moves from simple patterns to

complex and then figurative ones, showing us how syntax itself can operate as metaphor. In her final chapter, she explores this concept in more detail, demonstrating how "the syntax itself becomes a kind of simulation" with an example from James Joyce's *A Portrait of the Artist as a Young Man*: "He watched their flight: bird after bird: a dark flash, a swerve, a flash again, a dart aside, a curve, a flutter of wings." This is how writers move beyond "the arbitrary, the sufficient" to syntax that "seems not only right but inevitable." Let Tufte, and the wide cast of authors she has collected here, show you the possibilities.

WEEK 47
SANDRA SCOFIELD, THE LAST DRAFT

It is week forty-seven. If you are doing NaNoWriMo, the final week is coming up. The last time I did NaNo, Thanksgiving week was the point where the early morning and late-night writing time I had been squeezing in got squeezed back out amid traveling and visiting family and cooking and eating. If you are doing NaNo and have similar plans in front of you, remember that these are all good and important things too—just like your novel. Give yourself permission to take a breather if that's what you need. If you are still going strong, though, keep writing away and see how much you can get accomplished this week. I'm cheering for you!

Sandra Scofield, author of this week's book, *The Last Draft: A Novelist's Guide to Revision*, is rooting for you to succeed too. Scofield is a warm and encouraging guide through the wilderness of the revision process. "You can't do everything at once," she reassures us. "And you can't shrivel with fear thinking about the challenges ahead. You have to do the task in front of you, and then the next one. You'll get there by sheer doggedness. Perseverance is the best friend of talent." Amen!

Scofield is a believer in deep revision; this is not a book about surface polishing. She wants you to think of your first draft "as a canopy of writing, holding however many drafts it takes to get you to the place where you feel you have grasped the story and put it on the page. You have to know how it ends. You have to know what it means." Scofield's process in *The Last Draft* is to lead you on a discovery mission through your story. The lengthy second part of the book is a series of craft lessons, which she then asks you to apply to your draft. You aren't yet revising, but you are determining the work that you need to do and getting more inspiration, including from the work of other authors. You'll keep stepping back from the story and then zooming in to specific scenes. In the process, "the real book might appear in the margins of your draft."

After this period of analysis, Scofield leads you through a series of exercises to set up and then complete a full revision of the manuscript. Again, much of this work is about seeing the big picture; she trusts that you know what to do when it comes to the details of rewriting the draft. At the start of the real revision process, for example, she suggests completing three different kinds of summaries of the new draft before making a comprehensive, scene-by-scene revision plan. At the end of this first revision stage, she suggests as a final step: "Write a document that describes your love of your story. Reflect on the work you have done and all you have accomplished. Restate your resolution. Respect the process that is taking you forward." I heartily endorse this exercise. As Scofield says, "Don't skip this step!"

In terms of craft, *The Last Draft* will also teach you quite a bit. Scofield's method is to discuss a topic, analyze one or more examples, and then turn you back to your draft to see how you've used (or abused or neglected) this aspect of craft in your own manuscript. Here are a few lessons I thought were particularly useful:

- On summary, which Scofield argues (and I agree) is a neglected aspect of craft: Summary can be used to open or "link scenes in a sequence ... like stringing a necklace with some large stones and some small ones." When writing a summary, use concrete details (but sparingly) and indirect discourse (for example, "she thanked me and explained the necklace had belonged to her mother," rather than, "'Thank you,' she said. 'It was my mother's.'"). The goals is to give the reader "the sense of what happened and how it felt"; "all the grit is pressed out, and we are left with the flow of story, transporting the reader through time."
- On setting: Scofield notes that a frequent problem she sees among beginning authors is that "too many things take place in too few settings." Challenge yourself to reimagine some of your scenes in "a setting that in some way aggravates or emphasizes or contrasts with the conflict between characters."
- On backstory: "What often happens in novel drafts is that writers get ideas about the past while they are writing the ongoing present, and they get bogged down trying to invent, integrate, and balance these elements—making all of it up at the same time. They end up suffocating action with backstory. They lose the thread and the tension of now." To straighten this out in your draft, make sure every backstory element in your draft passes these three tests: "You need to tell it. This is the

> right time to do so. It has a consequence,
> emotional or physical, for the character."

The Last Draft will require patience, study, and practice. It's not going to take you on the most direct path to your next draft or to your finished manuscript. But if you can stick with it, you might discover an even better book along the way.

WEEK 48
HELEN CORNER-BRYANT AND KATHRYN PRICE, ON EDITING

It is week forty-eight. How's the writing going? Give yourself double credit for any writing you get done in these waning weeks of the year. There are lots of distractions and to-do lists trying to pull you away. Do what you need to do, enjoy the things that give you joy, and keep the writing going as you can. Don't add guilt or regret to the psychic piles you are carrying around. (Or just go ahead and burn those fucking piles to the ground right now.)

The only work I did during this Thanksgiving week was on my two long cross-country flights. In between, I spent time with my family, helped my mother move to a new place, and did a lot of cooking and eating. While I was helping my mother pack, she showed me a homemade library card (dated January 17, 1985!) she had found in one of her books. When my little sister wanted to entice me to pull my nose out of a book, playing library was one of the few reliable ways to get me to say yes. (My mother also showed me a handwritten "quot" from my sister when she was ten, promising that she wouldn't be as terrible a thirteen-year-old as I was. Now that I've run the gauntlet of thirteen with one of my own kids, I have a lot more sympathy both for my aggrieved thirteen-year-old self and for my parents.)

I read Helen Corner-Bryant and Kathryn Price's book, *On Editing: How to Edit Your Novel the Professional Way*, on my flight home while munching on Thanksgiving leftovers. It covers much of the ground we've seen in other books I've reviewed this year, with chapters on character, plot, point of view, dialogue, and more. Two things set this book apart: Corner-Bryant and Price create their own examples throughout, which allows them to clearly demonstrate their advice, and they provide two chapters discussing how to submit your manuscript and how to work with an agent and editor. (The authors are British, and their advice in these last chapters is supplemented by a US perspective from Michele Rubin.)

On Editing also features the best discussion I've seen of the familiar advice to "show not tell." This chapter is the last in the book before the publishing-focused chapters, and the authors use it to bring together all of their advice from preceding chapters: "At its simplest, the aim of showing is to bring the reader as close as possible to the action, allowing us to witness it first-hand and therefore delivering a more involving reading experience." It's a technique, but also a mind-set.

Here's a snippet from the authors' "before" example: "Sarah walked slowly along the dark, creepy corridor. Suddenly she heard a sound that made her jump. It was terrifying, and she was sure that she was in danger. She turned quickly, but she couldn't see anything behind her. The darkness was completely impenetrable." It's a promising situation, but the writing is as bland as unseasoned mashed potatoes. (I'm still savoring the taste of our Thanksgiving potatoes, made with butter *and* sour cream *and* cream cheese.)

Here's the revision: "Sarah edged along the corridor, one

hand clutching at the air, the other clamped to her mouth. She heard a scuffle from behind and spun around, squinting into the gloom. There was no point—even if someone had been standing a foot away from her she couldn't have seen them. She swallowed, her throat pulsing with the hammering in her chest." Better, right?

The revised passage encapsulates a number of the authors' lessons. For example, *walked slowly* becomes *edged*, a case where a weak adverb-verb combination is successfully changed to a stronger verb. (As I've discussed in other essays, however, please do not strip your manuscript of all adverbs! Any advice that tells you to eliminate an entire category of words is bad advice.) The word *sound* is changed to the more specific *scuffle*. Most importantly, *It was terrifying, and she was sure that she was in danger* is deleted. As the authors note, this sentence is telling us how Sarah feels rather than showing us: "Hmm, we think, this is probably scary for Sarah. But we don't feel scared." Instead, "let the atmosphere of the scene and the character's feelings come through in the action and description." The new sentence *She swallowed, her throat pulsing with the hammering in her chest* provides us with concrete, relatable details that allow us to imagine exactly what it is like to be Sarah in this moment.

In other words, you don't want your readers to watch your characters feeling; you want your readers to feel *with* your characters. If you've ever gotten feedback from a reader, agent, or editor that you need to work on showing rather than telling, then *On Editing* is the book you should choose to guide your revisions.

WEEK 49
BROOKS LANDON, BUILDING GREAT SENTENCES

It is week forty-nine. Here in my blue garret, the atmosphere is peaceful, contemplative. The next few weeks are busy ones, with gatherings to host and cookies to bake and a road trip to plan, but I've set aside a few hours this morning to savor writing this last essay of the year. If you are able to carve out your own writing sessions over these next few weeks, treat them with extra reverence. Relax into them and enjoy them. Give yourself permission to play with words rather than count them up. Go slowly.

If you want to try out some aimless writing experiments, this week's book, *Building Great Sentences: How to Write the Kinds of Sentences You Love to Read* by Brooks Landon, is a good one to dip into. Landon's goal is to teach you how to add detail and richness to your sentences by starting with a simple base clause and attaching words, phrases, and clauses.

There are three methods for adding material:

1. Connective: Starting with a base clause or kernel (in bold in the examples) and then adding information like adding boxcars to an engine. For

example: "**The girl raised the flag** and was proud to see it waving once again over the town square."
2. Subordinative: Weaving new information into the base clause through relative clauses or phrases. For example: "**The girl**, who had just realized she was the only survivor, **raised the flag**." Or: "**The girl raised the flag** that had long been the symbol of the resistance."
3. Adjectival: Adding words or phrases that modify our understanding of the base clause. For example: "**The** young **girl raised the flag**." Or: "**The girl raised the flag**, a triumphant grin on her face, the flag's green striped fabric tattered and torn by bullets, her bravery an inspiration to her compatriots."

Landon focuses primarily on the last strategy, showing us a variety of ways to create "free modifiers"—phrases, often set off by commas, that can be easily moved around in a sentence without disrupting the essential meaning. If you read my review of Virginia Tufte's *Artful Sentences* in week forty-six, you'll recognize the phrase. There is some overlap between these two books, and they make good companions for one another. Landon supplies the grammatical explanations that Tufte skips over, and Tufte's enticing banquet of sentence examples will inspire you to experiment with your own in ways that Landon's samples might not.

Landon makes the point that sentences have two different axes: they move forward in time, building meaning as they go, but they also have a vertical axis, which pauses the forward momentum of the sentence to add detail about a word or clause that we have just read or are about to read. Here's an example that Landon breaks down into different levels, starting from the base clause:

- (1) Cumulative sentences can take any number of forms,
- (2) detailing both frozen or static scenes and moving processes,
- (2) their insistent rhythm always asking for another modifying phrase,
- (3) allowing us to achieve ever-greater degrees of specificity and precision,
- (4) a process of focusing the sentence in much the same way a movie camera can focus and refocus on a scene,
- (5) zooming in for a close-up to reveal almost microscopic detail,
- (5) panning back to offer a wide-angle panorama,
- (5) offering new angles or perspectives from which to examine a scene or consider an idea.

And here's a nice example from Joseph Conrad's *Heart of Darkness*:

- (1) The great wall of vegetation,
- (2) an exuberant and entangled mass of trunks, branches, leaves, boughs, festoons,
- (3) motionless in the moonlight,
- (1) was like a rioting invasion of soundless life,
- (2) a rolling wave of plants piled up,
- (3) crested,
- (3) ready to topple over the creek,
- (3) [ready] to sweep every little man of us out of his little existence.

After walking us through various methods for creating cumulative sentences, Landon warns us about a few ways that long sentences can come to grief (hello, dangling modifiers) before turning his attention to advanced effects a writer can achieve using his methods. There are useful notes here about rhythm and about parallel structure and balance, but my favorite chapter in this section is about the "periodic sentence," which is a sentence that holds its meaning until the end.

Here's an example from *The Great Gatsby*: "Even when the East excited me most, even when I was most keenly aware of its superiority to the bored, sprawling, swollen towns beyond the Ohio, with their interminable inquisitions which spared only the children and the very old—even then it had always for me a quality of distortion." Landon renames this kind of sentence "suspensive," which I like because it captures both form and function. Henry James is famous for writing labyrinthine periodical sentences that, despite their beauty, tax the reader's powers of memory. But Landon shows us how to harness the drama of the suspensive sentence without drowning the reader in detail.

Throughout the book, Landon emphasizes that a writer doesn't need to remember or even know the grammatical terms that describe these sentences as long as they can embed the structures themselves in their brain, voice, and fingers. Think of this book as offering a toolbox full of strategies for adding (vertical) depth and (horizontal) length to your sentences. Once these tools become part of your writing brain, you will automatically reach for their rhythms to create detail and meaning, enriching your sentences. As Landon puts it, *Building Great Sentences* is not a "textbook that sets forth yet another set of guidelines or rules for good writing." Instead, "the chapters of this book are investigations, interrogations, explorations, and celebrations of the sentence and of prose style."

That has also been the goal of my newsletter this year—to explore what a great many (more than forty!) authors have to say about how to write, how to tell stories, and how to use words. I have loved the reading, but I have surprised myself by loving the writing even more. I hope these pieces have helped to light your way and pointed you to some books that will allow you to take the next steps on your writing journey. I'll leave you with these wonderful words from Anne Lamott's *Bird by Bird*, which I discussed way back in week two:

> Writing has so much to give, so much to teach, so many surprises. That thing you had to force yourself to do—the actual act of writing—turns out to be the best part. It's like discovering that while you thought you needed the tea ceremony for the caffeine, what you really needed was the tea ceremony. The act of writing turns out to be its own reward.

These essays have been my tea ceremony; thanks for joining me at the table.

BOOK RECOMMENDATIONS

As I pointed out in week twenty-six, there is no "best" book—no single writing craft book to rule them all. Humans are weird, idiosyncratic creatures, and writers are perhaps weirder than most. A book that thrilled me might leave you cold. The best book is the one by the writer whose voice you trust and whose advice you will take. That said, here are my recommendations for books that might help you work through specific writing quandaries.

You have writer's block:
Pick up Elizabeth Gilbert's *Big Magic* (week 6)—or, better yet, listen to the audiobook—if you need warm, empathetic reassurance that, yes, this is hard and, yes, you can do it. Take a look at Twyla Tharp's *Creative Habit* (week 19) if you need a tough-love, get-over-yourself approach, along with inventive exercises to get you unstuck. Try Natalie Goldberg's *Writing Down the Bones* (week 10) if you want to establish a regular writing practice.

You have questions about genre: Which one are you writing in? What are the rules and conventions for that genre?
Jessica Brody provides a clear, thorough taxonomy of common genres in *Save the Cat! Writes a Novel* (week 14), as well as specific tips for each one. Shawn Coyne's discussion of genre in *Story Grid* (weeks 7 & 8) is somewhat more theoretical but can be supplemented with blog posts and podcasts from his website, especially the resources at this link: https://storygrid.com/understanding-genre/

You consistently get stuck a third of the way into every manuscript:
You may have exhausted the creative possibilities of your original situation and now need to figure out the next plot steps that will carry you to the ending. Studying story structure may provide you the clues you need. Jessica Brody's *Save the Cat! Writes a Novel* (week 14) and Chuck Wendig's *Damn Fine Story* (week 16) both provide clear explanations of basic story structure. Wendig's book also contains a list of possible plot moves to help you move through the "mushy middle."

You want to write a novel that doesn't follow the traditional three-act structure:
In *Meander, Spiral, Explode* (week 30), Jane Alison questions why our stories so often follow a wave pattern of rising action, climax, and resolution and offers up a banquet of alternative possibilities.

You're an experienced writer and want to study the finer points of commercial fiction:
In *Writing the Breakout Novel* (week 44), Donald Maas looks at what separates great novels from merely good ones. John Truby's *The Anatomy of Story* (week 45) is somewhat too

prescriptive for my tastes, but he digs deeper into story structure than any other writer I know and is worth studying.

You are a pantser who wants to learn how to plot:
K. M. Weiland's *Outlining Your Novel* (week 28) provides clear, action-oriented steps for you to follow. James Frey gives concrete tips for outlining in *How to Write a Damn Good Mystery* (week 21), delivered in a sometimes combative tone that may or may not work for you. James Scott Bell's *Write Your Novel from the Middle* (week 29) offers a new way of seeing the overall structure of your novel that might provide a good bridge for moving from pantsing to plotting.

You are a plotter who wants to learn how to pants:
Dean Wesley Smith's methods in *Writing into the Dark* (week 31) may help you move more quickly from idea to execution. James Scott Bell's *Write Your Novel from the Middle* (week 29) may also help you start drafting with only a few key waypoints decided.

Your characters are lackluster:
If you can't seem to get the characters in your head to come alive on the page, go straight to Lisa Cron's *Wired for Story* (week 4), which is a master class in how to write character-driven fiction. Elizabeth George, known for the psychological depth of her characters, also has some excellent tips for character creation in *Write Away* (week 37).

Your sentences are boring, or you are bored writing them:
Brian Shawver's *The Language of Fiction* (week 24) is the best all-around style guide for fiction writers I've found. Don't start with grammar books (or with your old copy of *The Elements of Style*); start with Shawver. If you want to go

deeper, I'd recommend Virginia Tufte's *Artful Sentences* (week 46), paired with Brooks Landon's *Building Great Sentences* (week 49), which provides the grammar explanations and writing exercises Tufte's book lacks.

You've gotten vague feedback from agents, editors, or beta readers:
Jessica Morrell's *Thanks, but This Isn't for Us* (week 42) will help you identify the problems these readers are struggling to articulate, and will likely help you see other problems in your manuscript as well.

You've never taken a creative writing class and want to get the basics:
Janet Burroway's *Writing Fiction* (week 20) is commonly used as a Creative Writing 101 textbook, so it's a good place to start (be sure to get the tenth edition, published in 2019, for its excellent and diverse example passages).

You want to establish a critique or study group for writers:
Ursula Le Guin's *Steering the Craft* (week 25) has sound, practical advice on setting up such a group. For groups who want to work through exercises instead of or before sharing their own works-in-progress, the exercises in Janet Burroway's *Writing Fiction* (week 20) would be a good place to start. Groups interested in working on sentence-level writing issues should look to the exercises in Brian Shawver's *The Language of Fiction* (week 24) and Brooks Landon's *Building Great Sentences* (week 49).

You want to remember why you are doing this hard thing anyway:
When you get to that inevitable point where you want to

burn everything you've done and walk away, read Anne Lamott's *Bird by Bird* (week 2) or Walter Mosley's *Elements of Fiction* (week 38) for reminders about why writing matters. Or pick up *Why We Write* (week 41), edited by Meredith Maran, to see other writers discussing the pain and frustration (and triumphs) of writing.

BOOKS REVIEWED

Alison, Jane. *Meander, Spiral, Explode: Design and Pattern in Narrative.* New York: Catapult, 2019. **Week 30**

Bell, James Scott. *Write Your Novel from The Middle: A New Approach for Plotters, Pantsers and Everyone in Between.* Woodland Hills, CA: Compendium Press, 2014. **Week 29**

Bell, Susan. *The Artful Edit: On the Practice of Editing Yourself.* New York: W. W. Norton, 2007. **Week 12**

Bickham, Jack. *Elements of Fiction Writing—Scene & Structure.* Cincinnati: Writer's Digest Books, 1999. **Week 36**

Brody, Jessica. *Save the Cat! Writes a Novel: The Last Book on Novel Writing You'll Ever Need.* New York: Ten Speed, 2018. **Week 14**

Browne, Renni and Dave King. *Self-Editing for Fiction Writers: How to Edit Yourself into Print.* New York: HarperCollins, 2004. **Week 15**

Burroway, Janet, Elizabeth Stuckey-French, and Ned Stuckey-French. *Writing Fiction: A Guide to Narrative Craft.* Chicago: University of Chicago Press, 2019. **Week 20**

Casagrande, June. *It Was the Best of Sentences, It Was the Worst of Sentences: A Writer's Guide to Crafting Killer Sentences.* New York: Ten Speed, 2010. **Week 32**

Castellani, Christopher. *The Art of Perspective: Who Tells the Story.* Minneapolis: Graywolf, 2016. **Week 34**

Corner-Bryant, Helen and Kathryn Price. *On Editing: How to Edit Your Novel the Professional Way.* London: John Murray Learning, 2018. **Week 48**

Coyne, Shawn. *The Story Grid: What Good Editors Know.* New York: Black Irish Books, 2015. **Weeks 7 and 8**

Cron, Lisa. *Wired for Story: The Writer's Guide to Using Brain Science to Hook Readers from the Very First Sentence.* New York: Ten Speed, 2012. **Week 4**

Dreyer, Benjamin. *Dreyer's English: An Utterly Correct Guide to Clarity and Style.* New York: Random House, 2019. **Week 11**

Forster, E. M. *Aspects of the Novel.* New York: Harcourt Brace, 1927. **Week 5**

Frey, James N. *How to Write a Damn Good Mystery.* New York: St. Martin's, 2004. **Week 21**

Gardner, John. *The Art of Fiction: Notes on Craft for Young Writers.* 1983. New York: Vintage, 1991. **Week 40**

George, Elizabeth. *Write Away: One Novelist's Approach to Fiction and the Writing Life*. New York: HarperCollins, 2004. **Week 37**

Gilbert, Elizabeth. *Big Magic: Creative Living beyond Fear*. New York: Riverhead, 2015. **Week 6**

Goldberg, Natalie. *Writing Down the Bones: Freeing the Writer Within*. Boulder, CO: Shambhala Publications, 1986. **Week 10**

Hale, Constance. *Sin and Syntax: How to Craft Wicked Good Prose*. New York: Three Rivers, 1999. **Week 17**

Hardy, Janice. *Revising Your Novel: First Draft to Finished Draft*. 2016. **Week 22**

Johnson, Charles. *The Way of the Writer: Reflections on the Art and Craft of Storytelling*. New York: Scribner, 2016. **Week 43**

King, Stephen. *On Writing: A Memoir of the Craft: 10th Anniversary Edition*. New York: Scribner, 2010. **Week 3**

Lamott, Anne. *Bird by Bird: Some Instructions on Writing and Life*. New York: Anchor, 1995. **Week 2**

Landon, Brooks. *Building Great Sentences*. New York: Plume, 2013. **Week 49**

Le Guin, Ursula K. *Steering the Craft: A Twenty-First-Century Guide to Sailing the Sea of Story*. New York: Houghton Mifflin, 1998. **Week 25**

Lynch, David. *Catching the Big Fish: Meditation, Consciousness, and Creativity: 10th Anniversary Edition.* New York: Targer-Perigree, 2016. **Week 35**

Maas, Donald. *Writing the Breakout Novel: Winning Advice from a Top Agent and His Best-Selling Client.* Cincinnati: Writer's Digest Books, 2001. **Week 44**

Maran, Meredith, editor. *Why We Write: 20 Acclaimed Authors on How and Why They Do What They Do.* New York: Plume, 2013. **Week 41**

Morrell, Jessica. *Thanks, but This Isn't for Us: A (Sort of) Compassionate Guide to Why Your Writing Is Being Rejected.* New York: TargerPerigree, 2009. **Week 42**

Mosley, Walter. *Elements of Fiction.* New York: Grove Press, 2019. **Week 38**

Pinker, Steven. *The Sense of Style: The Thinking Person's Guide to Writing in the 21st Century.* New York: Penguin Random House, 2014. **Week 39**

Prose, Francine. *Reading Like a Writer: A Guide for People Who Love Books and for Those Who Want to Write Them.* New York: Harper, 2006. **Week 33**

Scofield, Sandra. *The Last Draft: A Novelist's Guide to Revision.* New York: Penguin, 2017. **Week 47**

Shawver, Brian. *The Language of Fiction: A Writer's Stylebook.* Lebanon, NH: University Press of New England, 2013. **Week 24**

Smiley, Jane. *13 Ways of Looking at the Novel.* New York: Random House, 2005. **Week 18**

Smith, Dean Wesley. *Writing into the Dark: How to Write a Novel without an Outline.* WMG Publishing, 2015. **Week 31**

Tharp, Twyla and Mark Reiter. *The Creative Habit: Learn It and Use It for Life.* New York: Simon & Schuster, 2003. **Week 19**

Truby, John. *The Anatomy of Story: 22 Steps to Becoming a Master Storyteller.* New York: Farrar, Straus and Giroux, 2008. **Week 45**

Tufte, Virginia. *Artful Sentences: Syntax as Style.* Cheshire, CT: Graphics Press, 2006. **Week 46**

Weiland, K. M. *Outlining Your Novel: Map Your Way to Success.* PenForASword Publishing, 2011. **Week 28**

Wendig, Chuck. *Damn Fine Story.* Cincinnati: Writer's Digest Books, 2017. **Week 16**

ALSO BY KRISTEN TATE

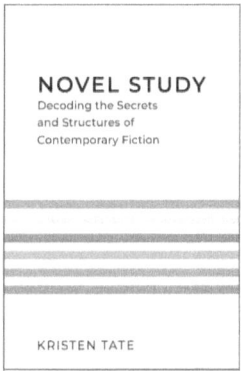

NOVEL STUDY:
DECODING THE SECRETS AND STRUCTURES OF CONTEMPORARY FICTION

It's not magic, it's craft

Most writing advice is designed to help you get from an idea to a finished draft, focusing on general principles and conventional wisdom that can flatten out creative storytelling and unique voices. In *Novel Study*, Kristen Tate delves into the techniques used by today's most successful novelists and translates them into practical tools you can use in your own work.

Through close reading and structural analysis of examples from a diverse range of contemporary novelists—including Ann Patchett, N.K. Jemisin, Tana French, Casey McQuiston, and Rebecca Roanhorse—*Novel Study* addresses common challenges faced by fiction writers:

- How to write a captivating opening chapter
- How to maximize plot suspense

- How to effectively manage multiple point-of-view characters
- How to create immersive settings and authentic dialogue
- How to craft sentences that resonate

Each chapter begins with a key question and ends with concrete takeaways you can immediately apply to your writing.

Novel Study includes nine full-color charts and graphs that illustrate many of the techniques discussed. You'll be able to see at a glance how successful novelists structure their narratives, manage chronology, and balance different elements of their storytelling.

Beyond insights and techniques, *Novel Study* offers tips and templates to help you build your own Novel Study files, tailored to the works and authors you admire.

There isn't a single way to tell a successful story. There is no secret formula or magic template that will make it easy to write a novel. But the right tools can unlock your creativity and lead to a manuscript that surprises you and delights your readers.

Novel Study: Decoding the Secrets and Structures of Contemporary Fiction

www.thebluegarret.com/novelstudy

ACKNOWLEDGMENTS

Thank you to everyone who read and responded to my newsletter, in which these essays originally appeared, most especially to Gail, who asked me if I had considered turning them into a book. (I hadn't!) Thank you to editing colleagues Rachel, Tanya, and Antonn, who cheered me on.

Thank you to Kelly Cozy for her eagle-eyed editing and sage advice. Any remaining typos are the result of my last-minute fiddling with the manuscript. Thank you to Rachel Metzger, whom I've been collaborating with for almost a decade now, for the beautiful cover.

Thank you to Sam and Gracie for embracing the garret and teaching me how to be a better human. Thank you to Rehmi for being ready to take any adventure and for believing I can do anything. Thank you to Rachel for inventing Fuck It Fall and seeing me through all the fucking Marches.

Thank you to Danna, who taught me that books have all the answers, and to Karen, who keeps me tethered to reality.

Thank you to all of my talented clients, who show me every day that stories matter.

ABOUT THE AUTHOR

Kristen Tate is a book editor who works in San Francisco, surrounded by cats to protect her from the cold, cold fog. You can learn more about her work and sign up for her weekly newsletter at her website: www.thebluegarret.com.

NOTES

Week 1

1. Khe Hy, "Frank Ostaseski: Have a Plan, Hold It Lightly," *RadReads* podcast, episode 34, https://radreads.co/frank-ostaseski-five-invitations/.
2. Laurence Stapleton, editor, *H. D. Thoreau: A Writer's Journal* (New York: Dover Publications, 2013).
3. Austin Kleon, "Thoughts as Nest Eggs," *Austin Kleon* (blog), January 22, 2018, https://austinkleon.com/2018/01/22/thoughts-as-nest-eggs/.

Week 9

1. Sue Brewton, "No, Charles Dickens Did Not Write That," *On Quotes and Misquotes* (blog), August 31, 2015, https://suebrewton.com/2015/08/31/no-charles-dickens-did-not-write-that/.

Week 16

1. Alexander Calder, *Moths II*, aluminum, steel, and paint, The Doris and Donald Fischer Collection at the San Francisco Museum of Modern Art, https://www.sfmoma.org/artwork/FC.797/.

Week 18

1. Julia Cameron, "Morning Pages," *The Artist's Way* (blog), https://juliacameronlive.com/basic-tools/morning-pages/. Also see her 1992 book, *The Artist's Way*.

Week 20

1. V. V. Ganeshananthan and Whitney Terrell, "Marlon James and Daniel José Older: Against Genre Snobbery," *Fiction/Non/Fiction* (podcast), episode 17, May 16, 2019, https://lithub.com/marlon-james-and-daniel-jose-older-against-genre-snobbery/.

NOTES

Week 23

1. Jocelyn K. Glei, "Who Are You without the Doing?", *Hurry Slowly* (podcast), November 6, 2018, https://hurryslowly.co/203-jocelyn-k-glei/. You might also enjoy the follow-up episode, "It Doesn't Matter What You Do, It's Who's Doing It," December 3, 2019, https://hurryslowly.co/302-it-doesnt-matter-what-you-do/.

Week 24

1. Strunk, William and E. B. White, *The Elements of Style*, New York: Penguin, 2005.

Week 28

1. Caroline Donahue and Frederick Barry McWilliams Jr., "#156 Meg Wolitzer," *The Secret Library* (podcast), https://www.secretlibrarypodcast.com/episodes/meg-wolitzer-156.

Week 34

1. David Cain, "How to See Things as They Are," *Raptitude* (blog), August 2019, https://www.raptitude.com/2019/08/how-to-see-things-as-they-are/.

Week 46

1. Austin Kleon, "Start Before You Think You're Ready," *Austin Kleon* (blog), November 5, 2019, https://austinkleon.com/2019/11/05/start-before-you-think-youre-ready/.

www.ingramcontent.com/pod-product-compliance
Lightning Source LLC
Chambersburg PA
CBHW031107080526
44587CB00011B/872